ASK
SUZE

. . . ABOUT INSURANCE

ALSO BY SUZE ORMAN

You've Earned It, Don't Lose It
The 9 Steps to Financial Freedom
The Courage to Be Rich

Riverhead Books
a member of
Penguin Putnam Inc.
New York
2000

ASK SUZE

——————◆——————

...ABOUT
INSURANCE

SUZE ORMAN

This publication is designed to provide accurate and authoritative information in regard to the subject matter covered. It is published with the understanding that the publisher and author are not engaged in rendering legal, accounting, or other professional service. If legal advice or other professional advice, including financial, is required, the services of a competent professional person should be sought.

RIVERHEAD BOOKS
a member of
Penguin Putnam Inc.
375 Hudson Street
New York, NY 10014

ISBN 1-57322-421-9
GEN-832

Printed in the United States of America
1   3   5   7   9   10   8   6   4   2

This book is printed on acid-free paper. ∞

Book design by Deborah Kerner and Claire Vaccaro

ACKNOWLEDGMENTS

I'd like to thank Melissa Moore for her help in compiling this book and Barry L. Wolfe, CLU, president of Centrelink Insurance and Financial Services in Woodland Hills, California, for his invaluable expertise.

INTRODUCTION

Over the years, I've found that one of the most confusing financial issues people face is the matter of insurance. With literally hundreds of different types of insurance policies available, it can be terribly confusing to determine not only the *kind* of insurance you need, but the *amount* of coverage you should have—which is often at odds with how much an insurance agent wants to sell you. That is exactly what I hope to address in *Ask Suze . . . About Insurance*—the two essential questions we all must pay attention to in order to protect our tomorrows from the what ifs of today: What kind of insurance do you need, and how much do you need?

I'm going to ask you to keep one thing in mind as you read this book: The point of insurance, basically, is to protect you if you have not yet been able to amass enough money to create protection of your own. Now I know that may sound overly simplified, but the fact is that many of us tend to have insufficient insurance when we are younger and too much insurance or the wrong kind of insurance when we are older. You see, when we have less financially, many of us tend to forgo insurance or try to get by with less than we really need, because it's harder to pay the premiums. But this can be a dangerous mistake, one you truly cannot afford to make, for if something unfortunate happens, it could be too late to correct it, and it just may be a mistake that your loved ones end up paying for, for years to come.

On the other hand, as we get older and have more discretionary income to spend on insurance premiums, or if we want to compensate for not having accumulated the financial resources we'd hoped to have by this time in our lives, we tend to buy too much of the wrong kinds of insurance. Do you need insurance when you're older? Absolutely. But you need coverage like long-term care insurance (which many of us can't even bring ourselves to think about) a lot more than you need that huge whole life insurance policy I bet you're still carrying.

We must be respectful of our money and the choices we make with it. That means you need to make it your business to understand the insurance policies that people will try to sell you. To that end, I will explain the types of insurance coverage that I think you need as well as the insurance plans that, in my opinion, you don't need.

As you read, you may discover that you haven't made the best insurance choices, that you bought (or were sold) a policy that you really do not need. Everyone makes mistakes, right? No problem, for you will also learn how to correct those mistakes. However, if this book makes you want to run out and change your entire insurance portfolio, or even a portion of it, I ask you to do it carefully and make sure that you have secured new insurance coverage *before* you drop your old policies. Your new policy isn't going to be any good if something happens to you a week before it becomes effective! Remember, your old policy is most likely better than no policy at all. So if you do decide to make a change, apply for the new policy, get approved, make sure everything is in place, and then and only then should you drop the old policy. I can't stress this point enough: Do not leave yourself exposed between policies.

Finally, it is *your* money we are talking about here, *your* financial life, money you have worked hard for, and I want to make absolutely certain it is as safe and sound as possible. To achieve that goal, I want you to think about insurance—the right kind of insurance—as an essential piece of your larger financial plan. That said, I want to make it clear that regardless of your age, insurance of any kind should not be used as a savings vehicle. Many of you still think of life insurance, for example, as an essential, something you will need for the rest of your life *and* a safe haven for your savings. But the truth is, for many of us, especially as we get older, there is no need to die with a large insurance policy among our assets. There are better places—and uses—for your money.

So let's begin by addressing the most basic questions regarding insurance, and step by step, we'll learn about what you need, why you need it, and how much you need, until, I hope, you'll feel confident and secure in your grasp of the available options, because knowledge is security, and security is our goal.

INSURANCE BASICS

What is insurance?
In a sense, all insurance policies are like a bet between you and your insurance company. An insurance company agrees to pay or reimburse you for the costs of your care or losses, depend-

ing on the type of insurance you buy, because they hope that over the long run, you will be safe and healthy and pay more in premiums than they will need to pay you for insurance claims. Usually they're right, but you agree to pay premiums and deductibles to an insurance company anyway in order to protect your assets in case you face major costs at some point. You are paying for the peace of mind that comes with that protection.

What is a premium?

A premium is the price you pay for your insurance coverage, whether you use it or not. Your premiums will vary depending on, among other things, how much protection you want to buy, how long your policy will last, the size of your deductible, your age, your health, and how often you make payments.

What is a deductible?

If something happens and you actually need to make a claim on your insurance policy, the deductible is the amount of money you will have to pay before your insurance company will begin to pay any benefits. Depending on your policy, your deductible can be a fixed dollar amount or a percentage of the total cost of your claim. In other words, you could be responsible for paying the first $500 or 10 percent of the total expenses for a given claim. Deductibles often have an annual limit beyond which you would not be required to pay even if you had additional claims. Charges beyond the deductible should be paid, at least partially, by your insurance company.

What is coinsurance?

Coinsurance is the fixed percentage of the covered fees that you are required to pay after your deductible has been subtracted from the amount of money owed on a particular claim.

In other words, if you had a policy that required you to pay a $300 deductible and 20 percent coinsurance, and you had medical bills, say, of $1,300, you would be responsible for paying $300 (your deductible) plus 20 percent of the remaining $1,000, or $200 (coinsurance). In this example, the claim would cost you a total of $500, and the insurance company would pay $800.

Insurance premiums are so expensive. Is there any way to reduce them?

It always pays to compare policies from different insurance companies. In general, you'll find that increasing your deductible will lower your regular premiums. But be sure that you will be able to pay a higher deductible if you have to; there's no point in having a $5,000 deductible if you don't have the money to pay it! This is a good example of the principle that money attracts money: If you can save enough in an emergency fund to cover a higher deductible, you can afford to take this risk and save money on your premiums. Also, if you can pay your premium once a year, rather than spreading it out over monthly or quarterly payments, you may find a savings of about 8 percent in overall costs. Please take the time to calculate what it is costing you to pay monthly or quarterly versus annually. I think you will be surprised to see the potential for savings. Another possible way to save money is by purchasing multiple insurance polices from the same company. It might look like a good deal, but be sure to compare the costs of other policies before you commit to a single insurer.

What does it mean if a policy is guaranteed renewable and why is this important?

If your insurance policy is guaranteed renewable, it means that the insurance company guarantees you that they will renew your policy every year, unless you stop paying your premiums or they discover that you lied about something on your application. In other words, if you develop health problems as you age, for example, having a guaranteed renewable policy means you won't have to worry about losing your coverage just when you need it the most.

How do I buy insurance?

Most people use an insurance agent to buy their policies. Agents usually have one of two specialties. Life and health insurance agents sell life, health, and disability insurance. Property and casualty agents sell homeowner's, renter's, and car insurance. Insurance agents make their living by earning commissions on the policies they sell you. A growing number of financial planners, accountants, and attorneys are also selling insurance these days. You can also buy insurance directly from the insurance company in many cases, but you will most likely still be paying a commission. You can also buy insurance over the Internet, through your place of work, through organizations, or through nonprofit groups to which you belong. How to buy insurance and who to buy it from will never be a problem, for there are always people or advertisements that will try to sell you all kinds of insurance. The key is buying the best insurance for your needs at the most cost-effective price.

My neighbor says I need to make sure that my insurance agent is independent. Is that true?

Absolutely! You have a smart neighbor. Independent agents, who are also sometimes called brokers, can sell you insurance from many different insurance companies and are supposed to get you the best possible deal. The opposite of an independent agent is a "captive" agent—a person employed by a particular insurance company who is only authorized to sell you the policies of that company. In most circumstances, you do not want to deal with a captive agent.

Why on earth would anyone ever use a captive agent?
Because they do not know better. People simply walk into an insurance company or are solicited by a particular company, and think that because the company is reputable, they will get a good deal. But as noted above, that agent is employed by a single insurance company and can only offer that company's policies. There may be far better deals out there but a captive agent cannot offer them to you. Independent agents can show you every policy issued by every insurer. This way you can comparison shop to make sure you are getting the best deal.

I read a magazine article about low-load insurance companies that made them sound pretty desirable. Do they offer good deals?
These are insurance companies who sell their policies directly to you rather than through an agent. They are supposed to charge less for their policies because they don't need to pay salaries or commissions to agents, although they often don't provide the same kind of services that a good agent could. If you are very knowledgeable about your insurance needs and are willing to do a lot of your own research, these companies may be worth investigating.

How can I make sure I'm getting the best deal on my insurance policy?
Only by comparing policies. For life, health, and disability insurance, there are several services that will research and send

you a free list of the least expensive policies (see the Additional Resources section at the back of this book). Sometimes, you can purchase your policy through the research service, but you should not be under any obligation to do so. You can also check the Consumer Reports Buying Guide, which offers evaluations of various insurance companies. But remember, when evaluating "the best deal," it's most important to make sure all your insurance needs are being met.

What do the letters CLU and CPCU mean on my insurance agent's card?

If an insurance agent has the designations "CLU" (charted life underwriter) or "CPCU" (chartered property and casualty underwriter) after his or her name, it means that he or she has taken some professional insurance courses, and passed the tests required to get those designations. All agents and brokers must be licensed by the state that they work in. If you want to make sure your agent is licensed, you can call your state's insurance department to inquire and, at the same time, you can find out whether or not there have been complaints filed against the insurance companies or agent you are thinking about using. (See the Additional Resources section for the general information numbers for state insurance agencies.)

Is there any way to find out if an insurance company is reputable?

After checking with the state insurance department to see whether the company has had a significant number of dissatisfied customers, look for an insurance company that has been rated financially sound by at least two of five independent rating services. The ratings by these services should be at least as follows: A.M. Best, A++; Standard & Poor's, AA or better; Moody's, AA or better; Duff & Phelps, AA or better; and

Weiss, B or better. Weiss will charge you a small fee to get ratings, but the other services are free (see Additional Resources to get the phone numbers and websites for these services). While high ratings are not an absolute guarantee that an insurance company is in good financial health, a lower rating should be cause for caution.

The first time I met with an insurance agent, I found it overwhelming. He had a really high-pressure sales pitch, and I was never sure if I bought the right coverage or not. My policies are up for renewal and I'm thinking about trying someone else. How can I have a better experience next time?

It sounds like you definitely need to find a new insurance agent! I'm guessing from your question that you signed something right in the office the last time, without comparison shopping, without reading the terms of your policies carefully, and without asking questions. Those are all mistakes, not only because you probably didn't get the best policies for the best prices available, but because they mean that you weren't in control of your money. Please take the time to read, compare, and question all the policies you consider, and don't work with an agent who makes you feel uncomfortable for taking the time to do those things.

HEALTH INSURANCE

Over the years, this form of insurance has gotten harder and harder to decipher and more and more expensive to buy. Nevertheless, it is still one of the most important types of insurance that you can have. If you do not have the proper health insurance, an illness or accident can wipe you out financially in a New York minute. So please pay special attention to the questions and answers in this section.

What would happen if I really needed medical care and I didn't have health insurance coverage?

The first problem with not having health coverage is that you will be less likely to seek preventative care, like an annual checkup, because you can't or won't want to pay for it out of your own pocket. If that is the case, in the event of a serious illness, it will likely be diagnosed later, and its treatment could be considerably more expensive, not to mention the quality-of-life implications.

If you don't have health insurance and you get into an accident, most hospitals will be obligated to care for you in an emergency, though ultimately you will be responsible for paying those medical bills, which could be substantial. One trip to the emergency room could put you and/or your family in debt for years, if you have to cover those costs yourself.

In other words, not having health insurance means that you could be deprived of proper care or not get the very best care you should have, and then suddenly find yourself hundreds of thousands of dollars in debt. Protecting yourself with adequate medical insurance is an act of self-respect.

I just graduated from college and I'm on a tight budget while I look for a job and find an apartment. I've always been healthy. Wouldn't it make sense for me to wait before purchasing health insurance, just for a few months, until I've taken care of my start-up expenses and then I'll get coverage through my job?

Not at all. Once you get a job, you may be able to buy subsidized health coverage through your employer's group plan, but it's not a sure thing and in any case you will have to wait anywhere from three to six months to qualify for coverage. Until you get coverage through work, and in case you don't, you must take responsibility for your own health and your finances, meager though they may be. Health insurance is vitally important, no matter what your age.

Does medical insurance on my car cover me for health insurance? Is that a cheap way to go if I feel I cannot afford health insurance, since I have to have car insurance?

The medical payments coverage on your auto insurance only protects you if you are injured in a car accident. What if you need minor surgery? What if you get pregnant? There are many different reasons you may eventually need costly medical services.

What is the difference between a group health insurance policy and an individual policy?

Groups of individuals who work for the same employer or belong to the same organization or association are often eligible for insurance that is sold directly to their employer or organization. This is group health insurance and it is what the majority of Americans have. The reason this type of coverage is usually cheaper is because employers or groups can often negotiate a relatively low rate and may subsidize part of the cost as well as extend coverage to spouses, partners, and children of their eligible employees or members. Those who work for small employers, are self-employed, unemployed, or unaffiliated with any organizations that offer this benefit need to purchase individual health insurance policies for themselves and their families. Sometimes, people will purchase individual insurance policies to supplement gaps in their group insurance plans, but if you have a comprehensive group plan, this shouldn't be necessary.

I have been told to buy a comprehensive policy, but I do not know what that means. What are the different types of health insurance?

There are essentially three different types of health insurance:

- Base plans generally cover most of your expenses when you need to stay in a hospital, when you have "medically necessary" surgery, when you visit a doctor, and when your doctor orders lab tests.

- Major medical insurance, or "catastrophic" insurance, pays the major expenses that you would have if you experienced a serious illness or injury.

- Comprehensive major medical insurance combines both of these and is, for most people, the most desirable type of policy.

The policy I have is called an indemnity plan. What does that mean and what is the alternative?

Indemnity plans pay a fixed percentage of your doctors' charges, whatever those charges are. What this means to you is that you may choose whatever physicians you prefer, and your share of the cost is predetermined. The alternative coverage is a policy that offers scheduled plans. Scheduled plans have specific fees they pay for particular services, usually at a rate the insurance company deems "reasonable and customary" based on a variety of factors, including where you live. Check to see what those rates are and compare them to what your doctors charge if you will be responsible for making up the difference.

Obviously, the indemnity plan, if you can afford it, is the way to go.

There is so much in the news about health care, I am totally confused. What are the basic differences that I need to know to make a decision as to what type of coverage I should have?

The basic plans that you have to choose from are fee-for-service health insurance and managed care. Fee-for-service insurance plans give you the flexibility to see any doctor you want at a price. You will usually have to pay an annual premium, a yearly deductible, and a copayment for each claim. Under a managed care plan there are small or no deductibles, small copayments, and lower annual premiums, but you can only see doctors participating in the plan.

Is managed care the same thing as a health maintenance organization (HMO)?

It would be more correct to understand that an HMO is one type of managed care. There are actually three kinds of managed care plans:

HMOs

In general, HMOs are the least flexible and cheapest of all types of health insurance policies. Premiums are generally lower, copayments, when they are required at all, are usually small, and preventative care services are almost always covered. In exchange, you must see only approved doctors and will need to get permission from your primary care physician before you see specialists or seek alternative care.

PPOs (Preferred Provider Organizations)

A PPO gives you an incentive to stay within its network of doctors by requiring only a small copayment if you go to a network doctor, but allows you to see any doctor you like, as in a fee-for-service plan, if you choose someone out of network. PPOs usually allow you to see specialists without prior approval but they do not always cover preventative care services and may have a larger copayment. Be sure to ask questions to learn what is and isn't covered if you buy this type of insurance.

POS (Point-of-Service) Plans

This is a type of open-ended HMO or PPO where you are encouraged to use network providers but are allowed to choose health-care providers outside of your plan, usually at a higher copayment or deductible cost. The major difference between a POS plan and a regular PPO is that the POS plan usually requires you to use a primary care physician to get referrals to specialists, if you want the insurance company to cover most of the expenses. Preventative care services are usually covered in POS plans.

Which type of policy is the best?

There really isn't a "best" policy. The decision needs to be made based on your own needs and preferences, both financial and medical.

I've heard that fee-for-service plans are too expensive and I'm crazy to use them. Is that true?

Not necessarily. Fee-for-service is basically another name for an indemnity plan, which offers flexibility at a price. You pay your premiums and a deductible, and thereafter the insurance company will pay the majority of your medical bills, no matter which doctors you see. Sometimes you will need to make up the difference between what your doctor charges and what the insurance company deems a "reasonable and customary" price for those services, even if you've already paid your deductible.

My sister says managed care is too restrictive and advised me not to buy into those policies. What do you think?

Remember, there are different types of managed care policies and they range in flexibility. What may be too restrictive for your sister, you may find comfortable.

So how should I go about making this decision?

If you have a choice, avoid rigid thinking about one type of plan being necessarily "better" than another. The type of medical plan that will be the most effective for you is the one that will meet your needs and the needs of your family.

Consider the following questions:

- How much can you comfortably pay in premiums, deductibles, and coinsurance?
- Do you have a doctor that you trust and depend on and want to keep seeing? Would he or she be covered under the plan you are considering?
- Does anyone in your family have ongoing health-care needs? Does the plan cover the services they depend on and have specialists to help manage those needs?
- Are there certain types of services or providers that you use regularly because they help you feel healthy, like a chiropractor, a psychologist, or an acupuncturist? Are they covered under all the policies you're looking at?

As usual, you'll see that if you can accurately assess what you want, need, and can afford, your decisions will be clearer, which means you'll be less likely to second guess your choices.

From a financial standpoint, what are the minimum criteria I should look for in an individual health policy?
Again, this decision is not only about money. The cheapest policy is not a bargain if it doesn't satisfy your unique needs. That said, at a bare minimum, you should try to have coverage that protects you and your family from financial catastrophe when you experience injuries, illnesses, or a major medical problem. Try to find a policy that is guaranteed renewable, has a maximum lifetime benefit of at least $1 million, and covers at least 80 percent of your doctor and hospital bills after you meet the deductible.

I've heard about these new medical savings accounts. How do they work?
If you are self-employed, employed by a company with fewer than fifty employees, or uninsured, you should look into a medical savings account (MSA). MSAs are accounts that you can contribute money to on a pretax basis, and then use to pay your medical expenses. Any money that you don't use in a single year can continue to grow with taxes deferred. These may be especially useful if you have a high deductible or copayment rate on your medical insurance.

I am on a really tight budget but I know health insurance is important. What is the bare minimum that I could buy and still be safe?
From a strictly financial point of view, you could think about purchasing catastrophic coverage. Catastrophic coverage pays for major medical and hospital expenses if you experience a

serious illness or injury. Premiums are usually very low on this type of insurance because you pay out of pocket for your usual expenses, such as checkups and even minor emergencies, and you will have a relatively high deductible if something major happens. Basically, you're betting that you will stay very healthy and that you will be able to pay for your basic preventative services, but are protecting yourself from financial ruin if you should need substantial care. But please be careful: If your budget is really so tight that you need to pay very low premiums, are you sure that you will be able to pay the high deductible in an emergency?

The insurance policy I'm considering has a stop-loss provision. What does that mean?

Although most major medical policies require you to make co-payments, they typically limit the total amount of money you would have to pay in a given period of time, usually a year. That limit is the stop-loss figure and it varies by company and policy. If your stop-loss is $3,000 per year, that means that you would never have to pay more than $3,000 (in addition to your premiums) on your health costs in any one year because after that $3,000 figure is reached, the insurance company will pay 100 percent of your covered expenses. Consider stop-loss provisions when you are comparing policies.

How can I find an affordable individual health policy?

As you will see, group insurance plans are often cheaper. It's worthwhile to explore other group insurance plans that you might be eligible to join. Professional and trade associations and religious organizations often have negotiated group coverage as a membership benefit. If you buy your health coverage this way, ask if the association adds any kind of administrative fee to your premiums. They may still be the best buy compared to an individual policy, but you want to make sure you know what you're paying for. If you buy an individual insurance policy, some insurance companies will offer modest discounts to people who are in good physical shape. Remember that if you're self-employed, you can set up your own medical savings account so that you are paying for your health insurance on a before-tax basis. If you do this you will save some money by not paying taxes on the money you spend on your premiums.

I just started my own business and, so far, I am the only employee. Am I stuck buying individual health insurance?

It is actually possible to buy group health insurance for groups of one, although not all insurance companies or states have this option and the specifics of the plans vary widely. One thing to keep in mind when deciding whether to purchase this type of insurance is that your own health doesn't matter in a group plan, because group plans can't reject members of the group for health reasons. If you have ever gotten your health insurance through your job, this is why you didn't have to get a physical before it became effective. So if your health is poor, a group plan for one might be worth considering, if it's available in your state.

Once I have an individual policy, can I keep it forever?

It depends on your policy. Guaranteed renewable policies can be kept forever, as long as you pay your premiums on time (although the insurance company can raise your premiums). Optionally renewable policies usually allow the insurance company to stop your coverage, but only within specific time periods, like the anniversary date of the policy. Conditionally renewable policies can be terminated by the insurance company for a variety of reasons (such as if you are covered under a group plan at work and you retire), but not if your health becomes poor. If your policy is optionally or conditionally renewable, check to see if your insurer is required to inform you when it is about to expire or be terminated, and whether you have an option to convert the policy to individual or individual family coverage.

So are guaranteed renewable policies the best?

In terms of medical insurance, definitely. You don't want your insurance company to be able to terminate your coverage once you've gone to all the trouble of finding a good policy, right?

What's the difference between health insurance continuations and conversions?

In certain circumstances, your eligibility for your insurance plan may change (you lose your job or begin working part time, you are widowed, you are divorced or separated from your insured spouse, you are too old to be covered under your parents' insurance, etc.). Both federal and state laws require that, almost always, in these types of circumstances you be given an opportunity to continue or convert your health insurance policy. Continuation means that you can keep the coverage, often at your own expense, for a specific period of time. Conversion means you have the option of converting your group coverage to individual (or individual family) coverage.

If I have group insurance through my employer and I lose my job, will I automatically lose my health insurance and have to buy an individual policy?

Not exactly. The Consolidated Omnibus Budget Reconciliation Act of 1985 (COBRA) requires most employers with

more than 20 employees to give you the opportunity to continue your health insurance for up to 18 months, at your expense. Your employer can charge you up to 102 percent of
their cost of your insurance, which sounds like a lot and is almost certainly more than you were paying in premiums before,
but might still be cheaper than buying your own individual
policy.

How do I know if I'm eligible for COBRA?

You should be eligible for COBRA coverage unless you work
for the federal government, the District of Columbia, or a
small employer (with less than 20 workers). If you work for a
small employer, you might be eligible to continue your health
insurance anyway, depending upon the state you live in.
Check with your state's department of insurance (see Additional Resources for phone numbers).

Do I only get COBRA if I get laid off?

Actually, you are eligible to pay for COBRA coverage in a
number of different circumstances, including if you lose your
job, if you quit your job, if your spouse who was the primary
insured member of your family dies, if your child is no longer
a minor, if you are getting divorced, or if you begin working
part time. These are called qualifying events.

My sister works for a small restaurant in town. The owner offers health insurance that isn't subject to COBRA because there are only about a dozen employees. Are there any options for her if she loses her job?

Many states require all employers to offer you the opportunity
to convert to an individual policy, but the coverage may be
more limited than what your sister had under the group plan

and she may have to pay higher premiums. Call the department of insurance in your state to see if she will at least have this option.

I'm insured through my husband's job but we're getting divorced. My company doesn't offer health coverage. What can I do?

Your husband's insurance company will probably require proof of a divorce (usually a notarized divorce certificate) before they will remove you from his policy. After that, you are also eligible for up to 36 months of extended coverage (at your cost) under COBRA, which your former husband, as the primary insured, must request for you from the insurance company.

I work full time and I'm pregnant. After the baby is born I would like to work part time for a while. As long as I'm still working for the same employer, why would I need COBRA?

Because you usually need to work a minimum number of hours per week, often more than half of a normal work week, in order to qualify for your employer's medical plan. The difference in cost to you, if you won't be able to pick up other insurance from your spouse or some other source, is something to keep in mind when you are determining a part-time schedule.

How long can I keep my health coverage under COBRA?

Usually for no more than 18 months. Under certain unusual circumstances, however, your coverage can be extended for up to 36 months, such as if the primary insured person dies or if your child is no longer eligible for coverage as a dependent. If you become eligible for Medicare (which makes you automatically ineligible for COBRA coverage) but your spouse isn't eligible for Medicare, your spouse can extend that COBRA coverage for 36 months as well.

What if I become disabled while I have insurance coverage under COBRA?

You can possibly extend your COBRA coverage for up to 29 months, but your premiums will rise for those additional months, depending on your particular situation (see the section on disability insurance to make sure you would be covered in these circumstances).

What if I'm working part time and using COBRA coverage but then lose my job? Can I keep my COBRA insurance for a longer period?

Unfortunately, no. You are only entitled to the COBRA because you lost the original health benefits and you haven't really lost them twice. The good news is that you are still entitled to continue the COBRA coverage until the original term would have ended. In any case, if you are paying for COBRA coverage over an extended period of time, you should continue to check up on other health insurance options that might be cheaper. It will be expensive to pay COBRA premiums for many months.

When I left my job, I told my employer that I didn't want COBRA because I thought it would be too expensive. Now that I've looked around, I've decided the COBRA coverage would really be best for the time being. Can I change my mind or did I blow it?

As long as 60 days haven't passed since your qualifying event, you can, in this case, change your mind. Just notify your employer as soon as possible.

I had great health coverage with my employer's group plan, but it's really going to cost a lot to pay for it under COBRA. Can I opt for one of the COBRA versions of the less comprehensive but cheaper plans that my company offers?

Not under COBRA. Your medical coverage must be exactly the same as the coverage you had before your qualifying event. Your employer has the option of allowing you to drop certain types of coverage, like your vision care, for example, which could save you some money, but they are not required to do this.

COBRA coverage costs so much money! Is it really the right thing for me?

It might not be. You need to consider your own health requirements and shop around for individual policies and group policies you may be eligible for, and compare them to your COBRA premiums to make an informed decision. If you have a preexisting condition, it may be difficult to get other coverage at all and COBRA can keep you safe, even if it costs a lot. If you're in good health, you may be able to find a better deal than paying COBRA premiums, if you're willing to do the research. But make sure that you compare services, not only prices.

I'm starting a new job but my health insurance at this new company won't start until I have worked there for three months. What kind of deal should I look for that would be better than extending my old coverage through COBRA?

If you are in good health, you might think about a short-term health insurance policy. These are indemnity-style plans (so you can usually see any doctor) which normally last at least one month but no more than six months and they have reasonable premiums. The tradeoff is that deductibles tend to be high, and they are often per illness, which means you have to pay that deductible each time you need to make a claim. The other thing to know is that most short-term policies will not cover a preexisting condition, so this is really only an option if you're in good health and probably won't require much health care during those three months, but want to be protected in case of a medical emergency.

My wife and I are getting divorced. My employer offers health insurance but we always used my wife's insurance instead, because the premiums were lower on her plan. Can I make her keep me on her coverage until the open enrollment period for my employer's insurance rolls around again?

You don't have to. In most cases, if you have lost your coverage under your spouse's group plan because of a divorce, you can start coverage under your own employer's plan without waiting for the next open enrollment period. Of course, you should check with your benefits representative to be certain, and, by now it should go without saying: *Do not drop your existing coverage until you are sure your new health insurance is in effect.*

My husband and I are both self-employed so we share an individual health insurance policy. Now we're getting a divorce. How do we decide who gets to keep it?

Here's one decision you don't need to make: Neither of you can keep a shared individual policy. Once you tell your insurance company about your divorce, they will terminate your shared policy and you can each re-enroll at the same company as individuals or you can go to different insurance companies.

I'm pregnant. My husband and I each belong to a group insurance plan at our respective jobs and I'm going to go back to work after my maternity leave. Once the baby is born, will her health insurance automatically be under my plan, since that covers the pregnancy?

Your baby might be covered through your insurance, but it has nothing to do with which company covered your pregnancy. It will depend on which months you and your spouse were born in. Whoever's birthday falls earlier in the year will be the insurance company you will use for your child. In other words, if your birthday is in April and your husband's is in June, your daughter should be covered under your policy.

My ex-husband has a group health insurance policy and I have an individual policy. My birthday falls earlier in the year than his does. Does that mean that my policy will have to cover our kids too? If so, can I make him pay for part of these costs?

Because you and your ex-husband have different types of health coverage, the birthday rule is not in effect. According to the National Association of Insurance Commissioners, group policies should always be used before individual policies to cover kids. How you and your ex-spouse divide the costs of any medical expenses, including premiums, will have to be worked out with your attorneys, but just because the insurance is in one parent's name doesn't mean that the costs can't be shared.

I don't ever want to worry about my children's health care. Can't my husband and I play it safe and both add our children to our health insurance?

You could, but it doesn't really make sense. If one or both of you have an individual health insurance policy, it's going to cost a lot of extra money to cover your kids on two plans. Similarly, group plans charge more for family coverage and tend to offer similar preventative care services. If you compare the plans carefully, you may find that you would not be getting much additional coverage, if any, for your extra money. Create real peace of mind and take that money you were going to spend on duplicate premiums and invest it for growth.

I'm in such poor health that I'm afraid I won't be able to get health insurance. Is there anything I can do?

High-risk health insurance pools guarantee health insurance to all individuals, no matter how sick you might already be. While pools vary from state to state, they are generally operated by an association of all health insurance companies doing business in the state. They are not doing this out of the goodness of their hearts, of course. They have been required by the government to offer coverage to state residents who have been rejected by other insurers for similar coverage or who are insured at a higher premium or with more severe restrictions than they would have under the pool. These pools are not perfect—premiums are often high and the benefits may not be adequate to meet your needs—but they do offer an insurance alternative for people in poor health. Call your state insurance department if you find yourself in this unfortunate position (see Additional Resources).

How do I know if I'm better off exploring my state's high-risk pool or just applying for Medicare?

Most state plans won't let you join their high-risk pool if you are eligible for Medicare or Medicaid, though some states do have high-risk plans for such individuals. Contact your state insurance department to learn what rules apply in your state. You then may wish to consult an attorney with expertise in elder care to help you make this decision.

MEDICARE, MEDICAID, AND MEDIGAP

Within the next decade, the average life expectancy for both males and females in the U.S. will exceed 80 years for the first time in history. Life spans have advanced by more than 25 years in a single century, and we can expect the trend to continue. By the year 2000, approximately 13 percent of the population will be 65 and older. By the year 2050, those over 65 will represent 22 percent of the population. Therefore, health care for the elderly is becoming a more and more important issue. What this means in real terms is that at precisely the point in our lives when many of us go on fixed incomes and no longer have the funds available to afford private medical insurance, our needs and costs for medical care increase as well. For a growing number of us, this is when Medicare and Medicaid will come in to save the day.

What is Medicare?

Medicare is the largest federal health insurance program and is the major health insurer for Americans over age 65 and the disabled. Once you qualify, you can use Original Medicare, which is a traditional fee-for-service health plan, or, in many cases, you can use a managed care organization, like an HMO or a PPO which contracts with Medicare.

What does Medicare cover?

There are free services in each state that will help you understand the details of Medicare eligibility and coverage (see Additional Resources). But, very briefly, if you are 65 or over, you can get a certain amount of coverage for hospital and doctor visits from Medicare. The type of coverage Medicare offers depends on whether you are covered by Medicare Part A or Part B.

MEDICARE, PART A

If you qualify for social security you are automatically covered by Medicare Part A. In most cases there is no premium charge to you for this coverage because part of the Social Security tax you paid while you were working went toward this coverage.

Part A generally covers inpatient-type benefits such as:

- Hospital care
- Skilled nursing facility
- Home health care
- Hospice care

MEDICARE, PART B

Medicare Part B coverage is not automatic: It is *voluntary* coverage for which you must apply at the age of 65 or later and for which a monthly premium, currently about $45 a month, will be charged. This monthly premium is commonly deducted from your Social Security check.

Part B provides for:

- Physician's services
- Outpatient hospital care
- Physical therapy and the use of medical equipment
- Ambulance expenses

Note: Neither of these policies provides coverage for dental care, vision care, or prescription drugs.

So I don't have to purchase Part B?

No. When you become eligible for Part A benefits, you will be sent an enrollment form for Part B. If you do not wish to purchase it, you must submit the form rejecting the coverage within two months from the date you received it. If you fail to do so, you will be automatically enrolled in Part B.

If I do not enroll in Part B at that time, can I do so later on?

Yes. You may enroll during any general enrollment period, also known as an open enrollment period. This is usually between January 1 and March 31 of each year. If you enroll during this time, your coverage will become effective July 1 of that year.

If I choose to enroll in Part B later, during a general enrollment period, will it cost me more than if I had enrolled at the time I became eligible?

What you need to know is that your Part B premiums will be increased by 10 percent for each 12-month period you were not enrolled in Part B. For example, let's say you declined Part B enrollment when you became eligible. Two full years later you decide you want to enroll. You will now have to pay a 20-percent penalty (10 percent per year). So your payments will be whatever the monthly premium would have been when you could have enrolled, plus 20 percent.

What percentage of my medical bills does Part B cover?

It normally covers 80 percent of the approved charges for covered expenses, subject to a calendar year deductible of $100.

What do you mean by approved charges?

The approved charge is the lesser of the actual charge or the amount indicated in Medicare's annual fee schedule.

Do you have to be over 65 to receive Medicare?

Not necessarily. You are also eligible for Medicare at any age if you develop permanent kidney failure or if you have qualified for Social Security Disability Insurance for any reason. Also, if you were born prior to 1909, even if you have no quarters of coverage under Social Security, you will be covered under Medicare. You can contact your local Social Security office to explore some of the less common alternate reasons that exist and whether you meet the criteria.

How do I get Medicare and when do benefits begin?

Once you apply for, and begin receiving, your Social Security benefits, you will automatically be eligible for Medicare when you turn 65. Coverage begins on the first day of the month in which you turn 65. So if you turn 65 on June 30, coverage begins on June 1. When you are covered, a Medicare card will be issued to you.

If I am over 65 and need to go into a nursing home, Medicare will automatically pay for it, right?

This is a huge and costly misunderstanding that many people share. Not only does Medicare not automatically pick up your nursing care costs as a senior citizen, they will virtually *never cover* them. Medicare has very limited coverage for long-term care. It is usually only available if you are in an acute-care hospital for three days before entering a "skilled nursing facility"—a facility that must be Medicare-certified—and Medicare must define the type of care you need as "skilled" medical care, not custodial care. Custodial care is what 99.5 percent of the people in nursing facilities receive; only about 0.5 percent of the people in nursing homes receive skilled care. Even if your care falls under this 0.5 percent, you are only covered for reasonable and customary expenses for the first 20 days; the next 80 days you are required to pay about $95 a day and Medicare covers the remaining reasonable and customary expenses. After those first 100 days, you are on your own no matter what. The bottom line is that Medicare rarely pays for nursing home costs.

If Medicare won't pay for me to stay in a nursing home, will it pay for my care at home?
Possibly. If a doctor certifies that you need to be cared for at home by a part-time or full-time skilled nurse, speech therapist or physical therapist, and the provider is Medicare-certified, you might receive some coverage. But be aware that very few situations qualify under these conditions.

My father still lives at home but he had a stroke last year and needs a lot of assistance, including physical therapy. What can he expect Medicare to pay for?
Because he needs physical therapy, Medicare will cover some of his expenses. But usually, if you are capable of living at home, Medicare will only pay if your doctor certifies that you need very particular occasional skilled assistance, such as physical therapy or speech therapy, and that you will improve with such treatment.

My father really needs help at home with things like cleaning and cooking, since he can't stand up for long periods of time. Will Medicare cover these services tem-

*porarily, since he should be able to do them again once
he recovers?*

No. Even if your father's non-medical needs are related to an injury, Medicare will not pay for home health care. You need long-term care insurance for this. Long-term care insurance covers care you receive in an adult day care center, continuing care retirement communities, and assisted living facilities. It will increase your premiums to have all these types of facilities covered, but if you have the protection, you will have more flexibility in seeking care later. (See the Long-term Care Insurance section for a more detailed explanation of this type of coverage.)

*My mother needs to go into a nursing home. What kind
of skilled nursing care will Medicare pay for?*

Not very much. If she has been hospitalized for at least three consecutive days within the last 30 days and if she'll be receiving skilled nursing care in a certified facility, Medicare will pay for the reasonable and customary costs of the first 20 days and part of the cost (less her copayment) for the following 80 days of her stay. Considering the numerous qualifications she has to meet even to get this paltry coverage, you can see how expensive nursing home care can become.

What if she can't afford those copayments?

If she has Medigap Plan C insurance (see below), it will pay for the copayments between the 21st and 100th day of her stay, if Medicare approves her stay.

What if she has to stay longer than 100 days?

She will have to pay out of her own pocket. This is when long-term care coverage becomes essential.

Does Medicare pay for any nursing services, ever?

If it comes to this, they will pay for a portion of hospice care, if you are near the end of a terminal illness. The caregiver is provided to ease the pain and suffering of the patient and his or her family during their last days together, and it will not matter whether you need the services at home or in a facility.

Can you explain Medigap insurance?

As you can see, Medicare will not cover all your medical costs. Also, like other health insurers, Medicare requires people to pay deductibles and coinsurance in order to receive their benefits. Therefore, you may want to buy additional coverage to protect you from having to spend a lot of money on these fees. Medigap is a type of insurance policy designed by private insurers to supplement Medicare coverage (although it does not cover long-term care). There are many different types of Medigap policies and they vary in quality and cost.

How do I know which Medigap policy to purchase?

The standard policies are referred to as plans A through J. A is the most basic (and the cheapest) and, generally, as you move through the alphabet, the number of benefits expand to J, which is a more comprehensive, and more expensive, supplement. Just so you know, any insurance company that sells Medigap coverage is required to offer plan A, with the basic benefits.

The most popular plan is C. You will need to decide which policy is right for you, but if you purchase Medigap, look for a policy that covers at least 20 percent of the coinsurance on doctor bills, hospital and doctor visit deductibles, excess doctor fees, and preventative care. Don't ever buy more than one of these policies, because they expand on one another, so you would be paying twice for some benefits.

Here are the basic features of each plan:

- Plan A pays the coinsurance required by Medicare Part A for the 61st through the 90th day that you are hospitalized in each benefit period and for the 60 nonrenewable lifetime hospitalization inpatient reserve days that you can use to extend your coverage; up to one year (over your lifetime) of your eligible hospital expenses after Medicare benefits have been used; the first three pints of blood you need each year; and the Part B coinsurance after your annual deductible is paid.

- Plan B includes everything in Plan A, plus it picks up the inpatient hospital deductible that Medicare Part A requires.

- Plan C includes everything listed above in Plans A and B, and pays for the coinsurance in a skilled nursing care facility during days 21 through 100 in each benefit period; the deductible required by Medicare Part B; and most of your medically necessary emergency care in a foreign country.

- Plan D covers everything listed above, *except* for the deductible required by Medicare Part B, and includes a benefit of up to $1,600 per year for services you would need at home on a short-term basis if you were recovering from illness, injury, or surgery.

- Plan E covers everything listed above for plans A through C, *except* for the deductible required by Medicare Part B, and includes coverage for up to $120 per year for preventative care, such as flu shots, cholesterol tests, or annual checkups.

- Plan F covers everything listed above for plans A through C, plus 100 percent of any fees you would be required to pay as excess charges under Medicare Part B.

- Plan G covers everything listed above for plans A through C, and pays 80 percent of the excess charge fees described in Plan F. Plan G also includes coverage for "at-home recovery"—that is, authorized care you might receive in your home, such as assistance with bathing, once you've been released from the hospital.

- Plan H covers everything listed above for plans A through C, *except* for the deductible required by Medicare Part B, and includes a basic prescription drug benefit, which means that once you pay a deductible, it will pay 50 percent of your prescription drug costs up to a maximum annual benefit of $1,250.

- Plan I covers everything listed above for plan E, plus the excess charges benefit in plan F, at-home recovery as in Plan G, and the basic prescription drug benefit in Plan H.

- Plan J includes every benefit listed above, *except* that it covers 100 percent of your excess charges (as in plan F, rather than the 80-percent coverage for this fee in plan G). Plus, the prescription drug coverage in Plan J is known as extended coverage, which means that after you pay a deductible, it will pay 50 percent of your prescription drug costs up to a yearly maximum of $3,000.

Will a Medigap policy cover any home or long-term health-care needs?

In certain limited circumstances, Medigap may cover some home health-care services but, as you can see, even the most comprehensive Medigap policy will not cover long-term care costs. Remember, the care must be Medicare-approved in order for the Medigap policy to kick in.

Are those letters in the Medigap policies related to Medicare Part A and Part B?

No, they are completely unrelated. If you choose to buy Medigap insurance, you can buy any policy you want.

If Medigap policies are standardized, why do different insurance companies charge different amounts of money for the same policies?

There are many different reasons for this, including the laws of the state you are in and the way the company calculates its premiums. It is absolutely worth your while to compare prices, and it is quite easy to do, since you know that the terms of the policies are the same: A C from one company should offer the exact same benefits as a C from another company, no matter where you live.

Does everyone need Medigap?

Not necessarily. And it may not always be the best buy, even if you decide that you need some supplemental insurance. For example, you may be eligible to participate in some group health coverage through the employer you had before you retired.

Can I be turned down for Medigap coverage if I am in poor health?

This is an important point. When you qualify for Original Medicare Part B, you have a six-month open enrollment period during which you can buy any Medigap policy offered in your state no matter what your health status is. This is the best time to decide whether you want to make Medigap part of your insurance coverage.

*My neighbor has part of her Social Security check paid
directly to a company, which she says she uses instead
of Medigap. Can you tell me more about this?*

She most likely is talking about what is known as a Managed
Care Organization or MCO.

What is a Managed Care Organization (MCO)?

In recent years a growing number of MCOs have contracted
with the Health Care Financing Administration (HCFA) to
provide both Part A and Part B services to Medicare beneficiaries. In the past such providers were HMOs, but as time has
gone on and many variations of managed care have sprung up,
a new kind of delivery system has emerged known as MCOs.

Simply, participation in an HMO or MCO works like this:
When you need medical attention, you can opt to use the
medical services provided by an HMO or MCO. The organization you have selected becomes the recipient of the premium that you have been paying out of your Social Security
check. In exchange for that fixed monthly payment from the
Medicare program, the provider you have chosen will take care
of your medical needs. This usually offers you a savings and
broader benefits than what you would get on your own. Some
HMOs and MCOs do not charge anything beyond the Medicare
premiums, and some charge more but offer more services as
well. Some companies offer additional benefits and therefore
eliminate the need for Medigap insurance. Getting coverage
via an MCO or HMO is, in my opinion, the preferred way to
go, because, in general, you can be sufficiently covered at a far
lower cost than through Medigap.

How come I haven't heard about these organizations?

If you haven't, you will. Expect to see a rise in the number of
Medicare recipients who are being served by MCOs. The gov-

ernment is mandating certain cutbacks in Medicare's fee-for-service payments, and is about to introduce many new options and incentives designed to encourage you to enroll in Medicare MCOs.

How do I choose a good MCO?

Please take the time to investigate as many plans as you can, but no less than two plans offered in your area. When you do, be sure to compare the following features:

- *Cost of care.* Although many MCOs do not charge premiums beyond the amounts you are currently paying to Medicare, some do. Check what your potential plan covers and how much it will cost you. Is it a bare-bones plan, meaning that it offers the minimum coverage required by Medicare? Are you willing to pay a slightly higher premium for broader coverage? Please pay attention when comparing potential out-of-pocket costs by looking at the deductibles and the copayments each plan offers.
- *Type of coverage and optional benefits.*
- *Choice of providers.* Many of you prefer to choose your own doctors, but you may not be able to do so if you choose an MCO that requires you to use its network. The MCOs that do not restrict your choice of doctors are known as Medicare PPOs, or open-ended HMOs. Be clear on this point ahead of time, so that after you have enrolled you are not surprised that you cannot see the doctor that you want.
- *Quality of care.* Find out if your MCO encourages preventive care by paying for some of those services. There are many nonprofit groups that monitor the quality of care that particular MCOs provide. *Consumer Reports*

has done some comparisons of Medigap plans and HMOs, so you may want to consult a *Consumer Reports* index before buying. See the Additional Resources section for a listing of other organizations that monitor MCOs and HMOs.

What are the main advantages of an MCO?

The most significant advantage is the opportunity to obtain full Medicare coverage, both Part A and Part B, at a lower cost. Additional benefits may also exist, such as services and supplies that are not usually covered by Medicare. A good MCO that offers additional benefits very well could eliminate the need for Medigap insurance or Medicare supplemental insurance, saving you even more money. Usually, paperwork is reduced as well because in most cases no claims need be submitted since all benefits are provided through the MCO network.

What are the disadvantages of MCOs?

The primary disadvantage could be the restricted choice of physicians. Remember, many MCOs require you to use network doctors and hospitals; if a wider choice is allowed you may incur higher deductibles and copayments when using non-network providers, just like a regular POS or PPO. It is also possible that the emphasis on cost could lead to a declining level of care in the MCO environment, if doctors are pressured to contain costs and handle larger caseloads.

Given the advantages versus the disadvantages, which way do you think I should go?

This will depend on the options available under the individual plan in your area, but on the whole, I would consider going the MCO route if the plan that you are being offered is a good one that gives you access to the doctors that you like.

What is Medicaid?

Medicaid (which is called MediCal in California) is a combined federal and state welfare program that covers medical care for poor Americans (and about 40 percent of all the people who are in nursing homes today). In order to qualify for Medicaid, you must be poor or medically needy, over age 65 or under age 21, blind, disabled, or receiving certain welfare benefits.

I've heard of people trying to "qualify" for Medicaid in a nursing home by putting everything into their children's names. Isn't this financially risky?

It is definitely risky, and not only financially. A major risk factor is the quality of medical services and the degree of personal choice and power that people retain over their lives as they get older. People on Medicaid have very limited control over their medical options, and the care available in a nursing home under Medicaid could be inferior to the care a patient would get if they were in a facility of their choosing, that they were paying for privately. Also, when parents sign over all their resources to their children, they become completely dependent. That can be emotionally and financially unhealthy for everyone involved.

Here are a couple of scenarios to convince you of this. If your adult child, who now owns your assets, is sued for any reason, those assets could be named in a lawsuit and lost forever. Another scenario: Your home is now in your daughter's name. She is tragically killed in a car accident. Her will leaves everything she has to her husband, your son-in-law, with whom you have never ever gotten along. Now your son-in-law owns your home. That is not a situation you want to find yourself in. Even if your daughter's will left the house to you, you might then have to pay probate fees to get it back, or estate taxes, depending on the value. (See *Ask Suze . . . About Wills and Trusts* to learn more about these situations.)

Also, depending on the value of the assets transferred, there can be significant negative tax consequences for your children. Please think about this before you transfer any assets. It just may not be worth it!

My wife needs to go into a nursing home. How do I know if she will qualify for Medicaid?

It can be frustrating to sort through the rules concerning Medicaid, which change frequently and vary from state to state. Generally, your wife will have to have a doctor certify that she needs the specific kind of care that nursing homes provide. She will also need to be living in a state that provides the relevant Medicaid benefits, be at least 65 years old, disabled, or blind, and have only a limited amount of income and assets. If you find yourself in this situation, seek the assistance of an attorney who specializes in elder-care law in your state or contact your local office on aging, which may be under the aegis of the state health department.

I live in New York but I would like to move into a nursing home near my daughter in Virginia. How do I establish residency so that I can meet the Medicaid qualifications of that state?

You just have to move to Virginia and plan to stay indefinitely. As long as you are in the state and have no plans to leave, you are considered a resident of that state and are immediately eligible for Medicaid.

What are the financial requirements for Medicaid?

Every state is different so, again, you should check with elder-care specialists in your state. Basically, though, the rules for qualification differ depending on whether you are married or not. As a married person, it's crucial to plan ahead because the consequences to your healthy spouse can be severe if you want to qualify for Medicaid, as you'll see in the questions below.

I am a widow. How much income can I have and still qualify for Medicaid coverage in a nursing home?
If you are single, everything counts. That means that all your income (earned or unearned) is taken into consideration in determining whether you qualify. This includes your Social Security, alimony, pension, worker's compensation, annuities, unemployment, interest, gifts, and dividends.

Now, in 33 states there is no limit on the amount of income you can have before qualifying for Medicaid. If you live in one of these states, you will qualify for Medicaid if the monthly cost of a nursing home stay will be more expensive than your monthly income. The other 17 states require that your income be below a set limit, which varies by state. If you live in one of these states, make sure you have a financial adviser with a specialty in elder-care law who can help you sort things out: Alabama, Alaska, Arizona, Arkansas, Colorado, Delaware, Florida, Idaho, Iowa, Louisiana, Mississippi, Nevada, New Jersey, New Mexico, Oklahoma, South Dakota, Texas.

What other assets can I have and still qualify for Medicaid coverage of my nursing home stay?
In addition to the income test, you will need to pass an asset limitation test, which has to do with your major possessions, like a house or car. Most unmarried people must turn over almost all of their assets to the nursing home in order to have Medicaid pay their bill. However, most states will allow you to keep your house if you think you'll be able to return there or if a relative or spouse is living there at the time you apply for coverage. You can often keep your car, no matter what it is worth, if you use it to get to work or receive medical care. Otherwise,

you can only keep a car that is worth less than $4,500 and investments up to about $2,000.

This is only the most general information. There are a lot of other rules about what you can and cannot keep, but the bottom line is that as an unmarried person you must give up almost everything you have worked so hard to accumulate in order to qualify for Medicaid coverage in a nursing home.

Once I qualify for Medicaid as a single person, what happens to my money?

Medicaid only makes up the difference between the cost of the nursing home and the value of your assets. Virtually all of your income, except for a small portion for your personal needs ($30 to $75 per month, depending on the state) will go to pay your nursing home bill. If you are expected to be able to return home within a given period of time, you may be allowed to keep a few hundred dollars each month to maintain your home.

As a married person, how do I determine if I qualify for Medicaid?

Again, rules for married people vary from state to state. In community property states (Arizona, California, Idaho, Louisiana, Nevada, New Mexico, Texas, and Washington), all of your income from any source, no matter which spouse the checks are made out to, is considered to be equally divided between both of you. So if you live in one of these states, half of all the income you and your spouse have is considered yours, even if, for example, most of it comes from your spouse's pension.

In any other state, only whichever checks are made out to you count toward your Medicaid eligibility. In other words, if you get a Social Security check made out only to you, Medicaid considers it as belonging only to you, even if you normally deposit it in a joint bank account with your spouse. If you receive dividends or interest on an account with both your names on it, that money is considered to be evenly split between the two of you.

As is true for single people, if you live in most states and the cost of a nursing home in your state is higher than your income, you will qualify for the Medicaid nursing-home funds. If you live in one of the 17 states with the set limit, you will need to fall below that cap. An elder-care attorney can help you figure this out.

Once I qualify, what happens to my healthy spouse?

He or she will be given a basic living allowance, a generally modest amount of money that doesn't have to go toward the nursing home, to make sure that he or she is not totally impoverished. Your elder-care specialist can help you estimate the amount that your stay-at-home spouse would be able to keep, because it will be completely different in each state, as are the formulas that determine it.

Do married people also have an asset eligibility test?

Yes, after qualifying on the income test, you also need to pass an asset eligibility test. Your home, car, and personal property are generally protected for your healthy spouse. Married couples can also keep some money in investments or cash: usually about $80,000, which sounds like a lot, but remember, this is all the stay-at-home spouse will have, aside from his or her income, which has basically just been cut in half. You can see that you have to lose most of your assets in order to qualify.

Studies of individuals entering nursing homes have documented that half of the people in the study on Medicaid were not poor when they entered the facility. They had to "spend down" their assets until nothing was left before Medicaid took over. (See *Ask Suze . . . About Planning for Your Future* to learn the steps to take so that you are never in this position.)

Is it true that even if I qualify for Medicaid, the state can put a lien against my property after I die?

Actually, yes. The 1993 OBRA Act requires any state that receives funds for Medicaid to have a recovery plan in place. More and more states in fact are actively starting to recoup Medicaid expenses. Not only are they getting the money back, but your family or other beneficiaries will have to pay it despite there being no way to prove that the amount of money that Medicaid is seeking from your estate was actually spent on you. So please be careful here and get advice from an elder-care specialist, since more and more states are starting to recoup their Medicaid expenses.

But you said my house was exempt from consideration as a married person! Does this mean that my healthy wife could find herself homeless?

No. Generally, while your spouse is living in the house they will not try to take it. Once your spouse dies, however, and the estate is left to her beneficiaries, the state could try to make a claim against it.

Can I just give my money to my kids and then apply for Medicaid?

Please don't do this! Medicaid is a form of public assistance and all types of public assistance make you liable for prosecution if you lie on your application or knowingly defraud the program. The government can look back in time to see whether you have given away money to anyone, including your children or any other relatives, in the past 36 months. If you give away your assets in order to get Medicaid benefits primarily to pay for your care in a nursing home, you may be making yourself vulnerable to this type of accusation and, if you are found to have knowingly defrauded the program, may become ineligible for Medicaid benefits for a period of time. Further, any professional financial advisers who recommend that you do this could be sent to jail or fined. Beyond the illegalities of such actions lie the more personal issues of the effect asset transfers have on your autonomy and your family.

So if we hide assets in our children's names and get caught, we just have to wait 36 months before we can apply for Medicaid?

You might think "just" 36 months, but you could also be barred for longer depending on how much money you give away. The state takes an average-per-month cost of what nursing homes charge in your area and divides that monthly figure into the value of the assets that you tried to hide. In other words, let's say you hid $200,000 worth of assets, and the average price of a nursing home near you is $5,000 per month. The state would divide $5,000 into $200,000 and get 40. That means that for 40 months from the date the gift was first made, you and your spouse will be ineligible for Medicaid.

If something like that happens, how does the state calculate when the period of ineligibility for Medicaid begins?

Some states start the ineligibility period on the date you made the gift and some states date it from the first full month after you made the gift.

What if I give away stocks; is that the same as giving away money?

Yes. Gifts of stock are also subject to the 36-month ineligibility rule. (If the stock was in a living revocable trust, you must wait 60 months before you can apply for Medicaid.)

If I don't want to apply for Medicaid but I have worked out a good combination of Medicare and Medigap coverage, can I rest easy?

Medicare and Medigap will certainly cover some of your needs, but if you really want to know that you have taken care of potential nursing home costs, you need to purchase long-term care insurance.

LONG-TERM CARE INSURANCE

As I said in the introduction to Medicare, we are a society that is getting older whether we want to believe it or not. Perhaps the most essential—and most often overlooked—type of insurance that most of us will need to have as we get older is long-term care insurance. This is the type of insurance that we would rather not think about. In this section, we are not only going to think about it, we are going to delve into it, and, in the end, emerge with you knowing that, when the time is right, you will need to go out and buy it. So read on and highlight those questions that strike a chord in you.

What is long-term care?

This is any type of medical, social, or support service you may need over an extended period of time. Elderly or chronically ill people may eventually need help bathing, dressing, taking medicine, shopping, doing laundry, cleaning, or getting around outside. These services can be extremely expensive and, as you have just seen, in most circumstances Medicare, Medicaid, and Medigap will not pay for them.

Who uses long-term care?

This is a frightening statistic, but the reality is that after age 65, most people have a 50-50 chance of needing long-term care. Those odds are higher than the odds of your house burning down or of getting into a car accident. You're probably covered for those events, right? Well, the average age of someone entering a nursing home is 84 years and the average stay is two years, nine months. That's going to cost a lot of money if you have to pay for it out of your own pocket.

I took care of my kids when they were young and I expect them to take care of me when I am older. What's wrong with that?

Many adult children do take care of their parents: Families provide 70 to 80 percent of all home health care and long-term care for older family members. But there are enormous financial, emotional, and psychological costs when families have to maintain an intensive level of care over an extended period of time. Long-term care insurance doesn't mean your children can't care for you, but it does ensure that you won't place a financial burden on your family at a time when they will already be experiencing increased stress and concern.

What exactly is long-term care insurance?

Most standard health insurance plans offer only limited long-term care benefits. Long-term care insurance covers the costs of long-term care services in a nursing facility or other institutions, and a variety of home health care situations.

Why should I buy this expensive insurance if I may never need it?

If you think long-term care insurance is expensive, you should compare it to the cost of a nursing home stay. Let's say you are 55 and will need to be in a nursing home at age 84: The projected yearly cost of a nursing home 30 years from now, if you live in middle America (assuming an annual rate of inflation of 5 percent), would be $148,176. Given that the average stay is 2.75 years, that would mean a total cost to you of about $407,484. The total cost of a long-term care policy if you started it at the age of 55 and paid each year until you were 84 would be $36,395. Look at the numbers: You will pay over 11 times more for the total cost of a long-term care (LTC) stay (if you only stay 2.75 years) than you did for the entire time you paid your LTC premiums (assuming there were no increases in premiums, which, in a good policy, is a safe assumption to make). Please note: In the year 2000, a stay in a nursing home in New York is already $150,000 a year. For you New Yorkers, think about what that cost will be in 30 years!

But why should I buy it, if I take good care of myself and think I will never need it?

Don't we all buy insurance in the hope that we will never need it? The truth is that you are actually more likely to use your long-term insurance policy than you are to use your fire or car insurance. One in 1,200 people will use their fire insurance, one in 248 people will use their car insurance, but one in three people will use their long-term care insurance, and it is the one insurance that you most likely do not have.

Should my marital status affect my decision about whether to purchase this insurance?

Everyone has to make the decision that is best for their particular situation, but here are some things to keep in mind: When you have to go into a nursing home and are leaving a healthy spouse behind, it is critical that they still have something left to live on. Price a couple of nursing homes in your area and ask yourself what would happen to your partner if he had to pay those bills and support himself at the same time. Most of us would be financially devastated. Now, if you are single, there won't be a spouse or life partner to be hurt if you need to use all your income and assets to pay for nursing-home care. But do you have children or anyone else that you wanted to provide for after your death? And is this really what you want to do with the money you have worked so hard for? By the same token, be sure that you and your partner will be able to comfortably afford those premiums, even after you are both retired.

Is long-term care insurance tax deductible?

Beginning in January 1997, if you purchase a long-term care policy that meets certain definitions established by the Health Insurance Portability and Accountability Act of 1996, your premiums, within certain limits, can be itemized as a tax deduction for medical expenses. These are called tax-qualified policies. Ask your accountant or an attorney or financial planner with an elder-care specialty about whether the policy you are considering would qualify.

My agent tells me that a non–tax-qualified policy is better than a tax-qualified one. Is this true?

In my opinion, currently the tax-qualified policies are not as good as the non–tax-qualified ones. It is the policy benefits and how you use them that are more important than the fact that you may be able to deduct your premium from your taxes. In fact, in order to deduct the premiums from your taxes you must itemize your tax returns. As people get older they tend not to itemize because they frequently don't need to. Finally, how many of you think your premiums will equal more than 7.5 percent of your adjusted gross income? This is how much your premiums will have to cost you in order to qualify as an income-tax deduction. Even if you buy a tax-qualified policy, make sure that you figure out beforehand whether you can deduct it or not, for in most cases you will not be able to.

If you won't qualify for the tax deduction, I think you would be better off buying a non–tax-qualified plan as long as the insurance company will allow you to transfer your policy any time you want to a tax-qualified policy. Check the policy carefully and make sure that the issuing insurance company will allow you to do this. Also make sure that if you do transfer the policy at some future date, they will base your premium for the new tax-qualified policy on your age of entry into the old non–tax-qualified policy. Then, and only then, you can go ahead and buy a non–tax-qualified policy.

Why is it important to be able to transfer into a tax-qualified policy?

Currently the verdict is still out as to whether or not the government will tax you on the benefits when you go to use a non–tax-qualified policy. Yes, you read that right. If the IRS decides to be stupid enough to do so, then it would be worthwhile to have the tax-qualified policy over the non–tax-qualified one. You see, in a tax-qualified policy, the government will not tax the benefits of those policies if and when you use them. But since the jury is still out on this one, and the non–tax-qualified policies are currently better, in my opinion, as long as you can transfer the policy later, you can have your cake and eat it too, no matter what happens.

How does the government know if I am using my policy?

Starting in 1997, insurers are required to report LTC benefit payments on Form 1099 LTC.

Which policy should I buy?

Until there is further clarification from the government, I would recommend that you get the advice of a professional tax adviser who is familiar with what is currently happening tax-wise and who can advise you as to which policy best suits your situation.

How do I know if I can afford to buy an LTC policy?

If you are single and are not able to pay your bills or are just making ends meet each month, long-term care insurance is certainly not for you. But if you are married, make at least $50,000 per year, or have assets (excluding your home and car) of over $100,000, or if you are able to save some of your income each month after your expenses, then you have assets that may make long-term care insurance worthwhile. The key thing is to be absolutely sure that you will be able to pay your premiums once you are retired.

Ask yourself the following questions:

- Could you keep this policy if the premiums went up 20 percent?
- Do you expect your income to increase or decrease in the next 10 years? If it decreases, will you be able to keep the policy in effect?
- How will you pay the premiums? From savings, from income, or will your family pay them for you?

I'm only in my 50s. If the average age of entry into a nursing home is 84, shouldn't I wait until I am around 80 to buy LTC insurance?

Please do not wait until you are in your 80s to purchase long-term care insurance; by then, the cost may become prohibitive for you. Not only that, your health may prevent you from being able to qualify for it. Like all insurance policies, you have to meet certain health requirements in order to purchase it.

So when is the optimal time to buy long-term care insurance?

I would say about age 54 as long as you are sure that you're going to be able to make those payments when you're 74, and beyond. Remember, these premiums should not make daily living difficult for you and your spouse, now or in retirement.

I'm 68 years old. Have I missed the boat?

It depends on your finances. Your premiums are going to be a lot higher than if you had bought earlier, but the cost could still be well worth it, if you can afford to pay it. Say your policy costs you about $3,000 a year, more than twice as much as if you had purchased it in your 50s. If you enter a nursing home at age 84, you will have paid $3,000 a year for 16 years, or $48,000. That's a lot of money, but what if you are in that nursing home for one year (a year and nine months less than the average stay)? Sixteen years from now it will cost well over $100,000 a year to live in a pleasant nursing home, more than twice what you will have paid in premiums. Everyone over the age of 49 is a candidate for long-term care insurance. I don't care how high your premium is, the total cost of your long-term care policy is going to be less than the cost of one year in a nursing home. So even at age 68, long-term care insurance still makes sense for you.

What should I look for in long-term care insurance?

The amount of money that your insurance policy pays for your care is the daily benefit. Policies generally offer between $50 and $240 per day for nursing care and 50 to 100 percent of home health care costs. The average nursing-care cost is $150 per day, or $54,000 per year. The length of time your plan will pay benefits is called the benefit period, which could range from two years to a lifetime. Factor in that average nursing-home stay of two years and nine months. Your premiums will be higher the longer the benefit period is. If you are between 44 and 64, consider getting a policy that pays a lifetime benefit. If you are older than 64, a four- to six-year benefit is probably adequate, but lifetime is always optimal.

How much should long-term care insurance cost me?

You should not spend more than 5 to 7 percent of your monthly income on premiums. This is a type of insurance where it really pays to compare prices, because policies vary significantly in terms of the benefits they offer. While you are comparing prices, look for a financially strong company that has at least a 10-year track record in providing long-term care insurance and in paying claims. Sometimes companies that are new to long-term care (or any newer type of insurance) offer lower premiums because they have not dealt with this type of insurance long enough to know how to price it accurately. You could wind up paying for their mistakes if they encounter financial difficulty down the road when you really need them. (See the Additional Resources section for my recommendations on good companies that sell long-term care insurance.)

My insurance broker recommended that I pay for an inflation option provision. Is this a good idea?

This provision means that your daily benefit increases a certain percent each year to help keep pace with rising long-term care costs. Some policies may cap this growth by an amount or by an age limitation. Other policies let you increase your daily benefit every few years by purchasing additional insurance at your current age rate. This is crucial. The younger you are when you purchase your insurance, the more time you will have for the daily benefit to grow. If you are between the ages of 40 and 70, the best choice will be the 5 percent compounded benefit with no age limit or financial cap, if you can afford it. After age 70, the decision to buy an inflation option depends on your particular situation. The 5 percent simple interest choice is less expensive, but a larger intial benefit may prove to be short-sighted.

What are nonforfeiture benefits?

If you decided to drop your long-term care coverage, nonforfeiture benefits could give you back some of the premiums you've paid in. Please keep in mind that while a nonforfeiture benefit might seem appealing, it can make your premiums considerably more expensive and, in many cases, is not worth it. You see, premium costs for these benefits are usually about 35 percent higher. If you can afford to pay the higher premium, take the extra money and invest it for growth on your own.

What is an elimination period?

Like the deductible in your medical insurance, this is the time period during your initial stay in the nursing home when you will not receive benefits. These periods are typically between zero and 90 days, and you are responsible for paying your costs until the period ends. Compare the premium costs between a shorter elimination period (say, zero to 30 days) and a longer period (60 to 90 days). If the difference in cost is not significant (it will usually be just $100 to $200 a year), consider buying the shortest possible elimination period you can afford in order to adequately protect your assets and estate. If you can afford it, I always recommend a zero-day deductible. Think about it—wouldn't you rather pay an extra $200 a year now versus your expenses of about $300 a day, years from now, for 30 to 90 days? If you can't afford less than a dollar a day for that extra coverage today, how are you going to afford to pay those payments of about $300 a day down the road? The answer is, you won't be able to, so go for the shorter elimination periods now.

Is long-term care the same as home health care?

No. When one talks about long-term care they mainly mean exactly what it says—*long-term* care—that is, care for a condition from which one is not expected to recover, a situation that is not likely to change. Home health care can mean long-term care, but in most cases it means care that is needed for a short period of time while one is recovering. Most long-term care plans that offer home health care protection will provide a daily benefit of 50 to 80 percent of your home-care coverage. I recommend a home health care benefit that covers no more than two years or 730 days. This is because in many cases if you need care after two years you usually end up in a nursing home environment anyway, so why pay extra for coverage that you may already have?

My husband is in an assisted-living facility. Would LTC insurance have covered this cost?

It depends. Most policies cover care in an assisted-living facility at some level. The definition of a long-term care facility may vary by policy, by insurance company, and by state. You want a policy that is flexible about where you receive care and allows you to have as many options as possible when you need them. While you want the policy to be flexible, you don't want it to be vague: Ideally it should specify a number of different types of facilities that would be acceptable to you.

What is a waiver of premium?

This means that if you actually need to receive benefits, you won't pay premiums. Check to see if there is a stated period of time for you to be receiving benefits before this waiver goes into effect. All good policies should have this.

What does restoration of benefits mean?

This is pertinent if you are in a nursing home for a period of time, and then you come out. If you are out of the nursing home for at least 180 days, then the policy will restore your benefits to their full level. So, if you had a four-year benefit period and had used up three years and now you had been out of the facility for 180 days or more, the company would restore your benefits back to the full four years. This way, if you end up in the nursing home again, you will be able to be paid for four full years.

I live in a state that offers a state partnership long-term care insurance. What's the difference between this and private insurance, and how do I know if it's right for me?

The fact that some states are starting to get involved in offering co-venture arrangements with specific insurance companies, called "public/private partnerships," to make long-term care accessible demonstrates how large the costs of long-term care have become and how important long-term care insurance is for older Americans. You need to purchase the most cost-effective and best LTC policy, which will depend on a variety of factors—and the state policy isn't necessarily better. They were set up mainly to protect the assets you have. Most partnership programs are for a particular dollar amount. Let's say you have a partnership program that is for $300,000 in benefits, and you go into a nursing home and use up all those $300,000 of benefits; then you have to go on Medicaid. Because you have a partnership policy, you are allowed to keep $300,000 of assets and still qualify for Medicaid. This is essentially how the partnership programs work. An individual policy with a lifetime benefit in my opinion is still the way to go if you can afford it. If money is an issue and the premiums of the partnership program work for you, I would not hesitate to go that way.

What should I expect from an agent selling me my long-term care policy?

Your agent should answer any questions you have, explain any terms that you don't understand, and be willing to explore all the ramifications of your policy.

You can expect the agent to help you figure out if a long-term care policy is right for you, or if you are not a candidate for it. You should expect your agent to select a company, policy options, and premiums that are best for your needs, to assist you in filling out all the necessary applications and forms, to submit the policy for you, to make sure that it was issued correctly, and to monitor and alert you to any changes in tax laws or federal legislation that might affect your long-term care insurance.

You should also expect your agent to explain to you why he or she chose the company that they did for you as well as the options that they are recommending. As with any agent, he or she should be patient with you and not try to push you into doing anything before you are ready.

My company offers a group long-term care insurance plan. Should I just sign up for that?

Many people assume that group insurance premiums are cheaper. Like medical insurance, while it's often true, it isn't always the case and there are significant differences between group and individual plans. With an individual policy, your contract is between you and the insurance company, and no one can change it without your consent. In a group plan, you still have insurance but the policy holder is a third party—in this case, your employer. Thus the insurance company and the policy holder can agree to changes in the policy or even cancel the policy without your approval. Most employer-offered group plans have longer elimination periods, limited benefit periods, fairly rigid benefits, poor inflation protection, no spousal discounts, and, depending on the state, are not guaranteed renewable. So check out the costs and benefits of an individual plan and compare them to the plan your employer is offering. Also, if you purchase a group plan, make sure that you can convert your policy into an individual policy should you leave the group.

How much should I expect to pay?

Again this will depend on the company you choose as well as the benefit levels, but here is an idea of what Continental Casualty will charge you for the following benefits assuming you are in good health at the time you apply:

A non–tax-qualified policy with a lifetime benefit period, a daily benefit of $100 per day, a 5 percent compounded inflation option, no elimination period, and a two-year home health care benefit at $50 per day will cost $1,057 per year if you are between 40 and 45; $1,337 per year if you are between 50 and 54, $1,550 if you are 55; $2,078 per year if you are 60; and $4,247 at age 70.

Will I always have to pay those premiums?

Again, in a good policy, once you start to use your benefits, your premiums stop.

What is the premium for an LTC policy based on?

This will depend on which insurance company you use, which options you select, and your age and health at the time of the purchase. What you have to remember is that your premium is based on your age and health at the time of purchase, and in a good policy should remain at that level for the rest of the time you own it. Keep in mind that most long-term care policies can institute a change in premiums as long as they have an across-the-board increase for all insured people within the state, region, or country who have this particular plan. But in a good policy this should not happen to you.

If I am married, is there any way that I can minimize the cost of our long-term policies since we're buying two?

Ask about a spousal discount, because many companies do offer a discount if you both buy your policies from the same firm.

Is it better to pay the premiums monthly, quarterly, or on an annual basis?

Pay your premium on an annual basis, if you can, because sometimes you will be charged more, as much as 8 percent more, if you pay quarterly or monthly.

If I know that I can afford long-term care premiums now, but doubt that I will be able to after I retire, should I sign up now anyway?

Before you buy a long-term care policy, you need to make sure that you will be able to afford these premiums for the rest of your life or until you need to use the benefits. It makes no sense to buy a long-term care policy if your retirement income, for example, will not allow you to keep up the premiums. Some carriers, though, have non-cancelable features, which have you pay premiums for a stated period of time and then guarantee no additional premiums after that period is up. With this option, you won't have to worry about being able to afford your premiums later on.

I just bought an LTC policy and they pay me on a reimbursement basis. I have been told I should have gotten a plan that pays me on an indemnity basis. What's the difference between indemnity and reimbursement?
You were told right. Your nursing home stay should be paid on an indemnity basis, not a reimbursement basis. The difference is this: If your benefit amount is $200 per day but your nursing home only costs $100 per day, with an indemnity plan you still get $200, while in a reimbursement plan, you only get what you actually spend, in this case, $100.

What determines if the policy will pay for my care or not?
The policy will pay as long as you qualify for benefits under their definition of qualifying. In a good policy you must only meet one of the following three criteria before the policy will begin to pay:

- *Medical necessity.* A licensed health-care practitioner prescribes and requests your long-term care.
- *Cognitive impairment.* You experience deterioration or loss of intellectual capacity due to an organic mental disease (such as Alzheimer's disease).
- *Impairment in activities of daily living.* You cannot perform one out of six activities of daily living (ADLs).

These ADLs include bathing, eating, dressing, transferring, continence, and going to the toilet.

How important are these qualifiers when getting a policy?

Extremely important. In fact it is one of the first points you should consider when shopping for a policy: When and under what circumstances do you get to use the benefits you have been paying for? Furthermore, this is one of the key differences between a tax-qualified plan and a non–tax-qualified plan. In a tax-qualified plan, medical necessity is not one of the qualifiers. This means that even if your own doctor feels that you need to have long-term care, you will not be able to get the insurance company to pay for it. In a non–tax-qualified plan, you would.

Also, tax-qualified and non–tax-qualified policies have different definitions for each one of these ADLs, so make sure that you ask and know the differences between them. For instance, in a tax-qualified policy the definition of eating shall mean: feeding oneself by getting food in the body from a receptacle (such as a plate or cup), or by a feeding tube, or intravenously. In a non–tax-qualified policy, eating is defined as reaching for, picking up, and grasping a utensil and cup, getting food on a utensil, and being able to bring a food utensil and cup to your mouth, manipulating food on a plate, and cleaning your face and hands as necessary following meals. Can you see how the non–tax-qualified plan is far more permissive? These definitions are very important when looking at a policy, whether or not it is a tax-qualified plan, so make sure you ask.

Is there anything else I need to look out for when buying a long-term care policy?

Remember that you must be relatively healthy at the time that you purchase long-term care insurance. Most policies no longer require it, but check to make sure that a hospital stay is not required before the insurance company will pay for your long-term care in any facility. Your benefits should be as comprehensive as possible: They should cover custodial (or personal) and intermediate care, at home or in an institution, including adult day care. Most policies require that such care be given by a professional health-care worker or a certified home health care agency. Informal care is a desirable option, but it may increase the cost. Your benefits should not exclude preexisting conditions, at least not for more than six months after the policy goes into effect. Once you begin receiving benefits, you should not have to pay premiums after a maximum time period of 90 days, including the elimination period, until you are on your own again. You should have to satisfy the elimination period only once, no matter how many times you need care. There should not be any changes in premium levels unless there is an across-the-board increase for everyone who carries the plan in your state, region, or country. It should be a guaranteed renewable plan and have a grace period, keeping your policy in effect in case you forget to make a payment. If you purchase a benefit period that is less than lifetime, make sure that the policy has the "restoration of benefits" feature.

If I buy a policy in California and then move to Texas, will it still cover me?

Yes, with a good company, the policy will follow you wherever you wish to have coverage in the United States.

How do I know if the company that I am thinking about is good or not?

I would only purchase long-term care insurance from a financially strong company that has been in the business of selling long-term care coverage for at least 10 years or longer. They should be licensed in all 50 states and have a top rating from the insurance raters (see Additional Resources for the names and numbers of the ratings services). I would check their history to make sure that they have not had many increases in premium levels over the years to existing policy holders. Finally, they should be competitive in the prices of their policies. Check them out carefully!

CAR INSURANCE

Most of us know a little something about car insurance, probably more than we know about our medical insurance. Why? Because we are required by the state we live in to have certain types of car coverage. However, just because the state mandates a certain amount of car insurance doesn't mean that it's enough. And, as with other types of insurance, agents are only too happy to sell us more than we need. In this section, we'll hope to clarify what you have or haven't got from what you need.

What are the different kinds of standard coverage I can get for my car?

There are four types of protection in standard car insurance—auto liability, medical payments, collision, and comprehensive coverage.

Auto liability coverage protects you if you cause an accident. It has two parts. Bodily injury liability pays the expenses of anyone injured in the accident. There is no deductible and while most states require that you have a minimum amount of liability coverage, this minimum may not be adequate if you cause a serious accident and get sued for pain and suffering in addition to the material losses. Bodily injury liability coverage will protect your assets. Property damage liability pays the repair expenses if you accidentally damage somebody else's property (like another person's car, or their house) with your car.

Medical payments coverage will pay for your expenses and the expenses of your passengers if you experience a serious injury in a car crash, whether you caused the accident or not.

Collision insurance is not required by the state. It protects your car in the event of an accident, among other things, whether you cause the accident or not. If your car is valuable, this might make sense. You can choose whether or not to have a deductible.

Comprehensive insurance, which is also optional, pays for the repair or replacement of your car if it is damaged by a fire, a falling object, earthquake, flood, theft, vandalism, or other type of non-auto accident.

I keep seeing all those numbers that look like dates when I hear about auto liability. What does, say, 30/50/20 mean?

These numbers refer to the limits of your liability policy in a particular accident. If you have these particular numbers, it means you have $30,000 in bodily injury coverage per person, $50,000 in bodily injury coverage per accident, and $20,000 in coverage for property damage.

How much liability coverage should I have?

Standard minimum recommendations for homeowners and people with more assets are at least $100,000 in bodily injury coverage per person, $300,000 in bodily injury coverage per accident, and $50,000 in property damage liability. Those with fewer assets should consider $15,000 in bodily injury coverage per person, $30,000 in bodily injury coverage per accident, and $10,000 in property damage liability.

Can my whole family and all of my cars be covered by one policy?

Yes, usually, although they don't have to be if you don't want to set it up that way. Generally, eligible cars are any four-wheel vehicles owned by an individual or married couple, or leased under contract for at least six months. If one of you has a motorcycle or a motor home, for example, you may have to purchase additional coverage.

Apparently I live in a no-fault state. What does this mean and do I need liability coverage?

Most states use no-fault auto insurance systems and other states use traditional third-party systems to settle claims. No-fault states require drivers and their insurance companies to pay for their own costs after a car accident, whether they were responsible or not. But you still may need liability insurance, because if you cause an accident and the costs to the other injured people are above a certain threshold, they can still sue you. If they win a judgment against you and you don't have sufficient liability coverage, the difference may have to come out of your pocket if you have it. In a state with a traditional third-party system, or a "fault" state, your insurance company only needs to pay your claim if you can prove that you did not cause the accident.

Is the medical payments coverage required?

No-fault states typically require you to buy this type of coverage, while fault states do not. An argument for buying this type of coverage anyway is that this insurance would pay no matter who caused the accident.

Couldn't my medical insurance pay for this?
You're getting insurance-smart, now that you are on the lookout for duplicate coverage! You are correct, your medical insurance might cover you in such a circumstance, but it will not cover any passengers who are not covered by your health-care policy.

So, can I use this as a kind of cheap medical coverage?
I don't recommend this. There are many other reasons that you might need medical care aside from being injured in a car accident.

How do I know how much collision and comprehensive coverage I need?
This is generally the more expensive part of car insurance. It is optional in all states, although if you leased your car or took out a loan to buy it, the dealer or bank that loaned you the money probably required you to purchase it. Most companies have vehicle pricing services. Blue-book valuations are not used very much. Most companies will insure for the price you paid for the car, as long as it was a reasonable cost. As usual, if the deductible is higher, you can reduce the price of the premiums.

Should my car insurance reimburse me for my replacement costs or for the actual cash value of my car if it's stolen or damaged?
It will cost you more to have replacement cost coverage, but it may be worthwhile because it will replace or repair your car without deducting for its depreciation. Actual cash value policies only pay you for the value of the car at the time it is stolen or damaged, which is reduced to account for depreciation.

What if my car gets damaged in an accident by a driver with no insurance? Do I have to pay for everything myself?

There is insurance you can purchase called uninsured motorists coverage that would protect you in these circumstances. (There is also uninsured motorist property damage and a collision deductible waiver.) Some states require you to have this coverage; it protects you if an uninsured driver hits your car and you have medical bills. There is also something called underinsured motorists coverage, which makes up some of the difference if a driver hits you who has some, but not adequate, insurance. In other words, you can make a claim on your own insurance policy if the person who hits your car doesn't have any insurance for you to make a claim on.

How much underinsured or uninsured motorists coverage should I purchase?

You normally can't have more underinsured or uninsured coverage than the liability policy that you carry (although you can have less). Therefore, if you purchase a 100/300 liability policy, that's the most coverage of this type you can have on the other policies.

How do I know how much car insurance I really need?

The state you live in and, if you borrow money to buy your car, the lending institution will require you to have certain kinds of coverage. Basic policies usually include some combination of liability, collision, comprehensive, uninsured or underinsured motorist, and medical payments coverage. As for what level of coverage you need, consider your personal situation in order to figure out what will make you feel safe: Is your car brand new or old? How much would it cost you to replace it? Do you have the resources to pay your medical bills and car repairs? Do you have valuable assets you want to protect?

Will my car insurance pay for the cost of a towing service if I break down on the road?

It might, but in order to get this you may have to add coverage for towing and labor. This is usually pretty inexpensive. Ask your agent how much this would increase your premium and compare it to how much it would cost you to join your state's AAA organization, which provides various towing and accident services.

When my sister got into an accident a few years ago, her insurance company paid for her to rent a temporary car. My insurance company says I don't have that kind of coverage. Why?

If it's not in your policy already and you want this coverage, you need to purchase a supplemental rental reimbursement provision. This coverage will pay for the cost of renting a car while yours is stolen or being repaired. Sometimes this is included in augmented insurance policies, but usually you have to add it separately to your policy. Like towing and labor coverage, this addition shouldn't increase your premiums very much, but ask your agent and compare prices.

I just moved from Georgia to Maine. My old car insurance policy only had a month left on it, so I figure I'll buy coverage in my new state and just let the old one lapse. Is that okay?

Absolutely not! Even though you don't have much time left on the old policy, you have to send written notice to your insurance company, telling them that you don't want to renew it. Otherwise, they will send you a bill for your next premium (to your old address, probably) and if you don't pay it, they will cancel your policy. But here's what happens next: That cancellation can go on your credit report, making it seem like you don't pay your premiums in a timely way. So take the time to send your old insurance company a letter.

Many states will require that you show your old insurance company proof of a new car insurance policy (a photocopy of your new insurance ID card is usually fine) before they can cancel your old policy. If your old company does this, don't necessarily take it personally or think that they're giving you a hard time about dropping the coverage. Finally, you might get some money back, so don't let laziness cheat you out of some hard-earned cash.

I moved from Florida to California, and I cannot believe how much more the insurance for the same car is going to cost me. Can I just leave my old Florida address on the policy and get away with it?

It might seem tempting, but this is called insurance fraud. If your insurance company finds out that you have lied to them, they may not honor your policy and you could even be liable for criminal prosecution.

I moved to a different part of town and my insurance premiums are going to go through the roof! A good friend still lives at my old address. Do I have to tell the insurance company that I moved?

You certainly do. The reason your premiums are higher is because statistically, the insurance company thinks that it is more likely that drivers in your new neighborhood will need to have a claim paid out. It might not seem fair, but what you are proposing is maintaining a false address, which is a form of insurance fraud. Don't risk it.

My son just turned 16 and got his driver's license. My car insurance premiums are going to increase like mad if I add him to my policy. Is there anything else I can do?

If your son is going to drive, he's got to have insurance, and insurance companies know that young drivers are risky drivers, so they charge you high rates to protect themselves. If your son isn't going to be taking his car to school every day, you can try to have him classified as an occasional driver, although not all companies will allow you to do this. Many companies do offer modest discounts if he has good grades or has taken a particular type of driver's education course, so ask your agent about these rules. Finally, if you want to save on car insurance costs, not only should you not buy your son a new car, you should have him driving the oldest and cheapest car you own. As long, that is, as it's a safe car—saving money on your premiums isn't everything!

Do I have to put my kids on my car insurance policy? Couldn't I make them get their own?

You could, but you won't save money. In general, it will be more expensive for your teenager to have his own individual car insurance than to increase the premiums on your family policy. If you want your son to contribute all or part of his car insurance costs, he can reimburse you for the increase in your premiums as easily as paying his own, higher premiums to an insurance company on his own policy.

Also, some states will require you to sign something called a named driver exclusion if you choose not to add your teenage children to your car insurance. If you sign one of these, you will be saying, in this case, that your son, specifically, is not covered on your policy and that you agree to be completely liable if he has an accident in one of your cars.

I got a ticket for driving under the influence and now my insurance costs have gone through the roof. Is there anything that I can do?

If you have been convicted of DUI you should immediately find out which defensive driving courses your insurance company approves of, and take one of them. In many cases, this will reduce your premiums to some degree, although they will still be higher than they were before your conviction. After that, you just need to make sure that you maintain a good clean driving record and remind your insurance company about it after a year has passed. Over time, your premiums should come down again.

Is there any way to reduce my auto insurance costs?

The premiums on your car insurance are based on, among other things, your age, your gender, where you live, the type of car you drive, and your driving record. However, there are a surprising number of small discounts that it is possible to negotiate. When you price different car insurance policies, make sure the agent knows if you have a clean driving record, because some companies give discounts to drivers who have no violations in their past. Most insurance companies reduce your premiums based on a combination of your age, sex, and marital status. (Twenty-five is the general rule for single women and married men; 30 is the general rule for single men. Married women are often eligible for the lower rate no matter what their age.) If you are in college or even graduate school and get good grades, some insurance companies will offer you small discounts, even for a few years past graduation. You can check with your company to see how they do it; some demand a GPA of 3.0 or higher, some want a dean's list, others want to know that you are in the top 20 percent of your class. Ask your insurance agent for a list of cars that are considered "lower risk" and make sure that your agent knows that your car has air bags and other special safety features, like an alarm system or anti-lock brakes, if it does. Finally, if there are multiple cars in your house, see if you are entitled to a multiple-car discount.

These discounts might seem arbitrary, but they aren't. All the discount-qualifying characteristics mentioned above are statistically associated with drivers who have fewer accidents.

Are there any other discounts on car insurance I should know about?

Just the general ones: If you purchase your insurance for your house and your car from the same company or agent, that might make you eligible for a multi-policy discount. As usual, if you have a higher deductible, you can lower the cost of your premiums. Just make sure that you will be able to pay that deductible if you need to.

If my friend drives my car and gets into an accident, will my insurance policy still be effective?

If you loan your car every once in a while, your insurance policy should probably still cover an accident. Rates generally do not increase if a friend is involved in an accident while driving your car.

When I rent cars, I'm never sure if I should pay for the rental car liability or collision insurance. What do you think?

I think you absolutely need liability coverage on a rental car, but that you often don't need to buy it from the rental company. Many comprehensive auto liability policies cover you when you rent a car. Check to make sure that yours does and then don't duplicate this coverage at the rental counter. Your car insurance may also cover comprehensive collision in a rental car, so check that out too.

Does my credit card cover the insurance that I need for a rental car?

Your credit card may provide such coverage as long as you use it to pay for the car rental. If you pay for a rental car with an American Express green card, for example, and you are not a student, you will be covered for collision and damage, but not liability. Do some research with your credit card company; the chances are that you've got this covered.

DISABILITY INSURANCE

We are more likely to consider how to take care of our families after we die than we are to think about how we would take care of ourselves and our families if we became disabled. Just think about it—if you were injured so severely that you could no longer work, how would you pay your bills? In a financial sense, it's potentially more problematic than dying, because not only can you not work, but your expenses may be higher than they were before, depending on what kind of care and services you need to accommodate your disability.

What is disability insurance and who needs it?

If you were seriously ill or injured, disability insurance replaces a portion of the salary you were making before you became disabled and unable to work. Single and self-employed people should seriously consider disability policies if there would not be financial support from another source if you became so sick or injured that you were unable to work. Even if you have a partner who could make up some of your income, you need to consider whether you and your family could survive comfortably without your salary.

How is disability defined?

A disability is defined as a limitation of your physical or mental ability to work resulting from sickness or injury. It may be partial, in which case you are unable to perform certain job functions, or total, in which case you are unable to work at all.

Is disability insurance the same thing as worker's compensation?

No. Worker's compensation protects you if you are injured while performing your job. Disability insurance is a form of health insurance that replaces all or part of your income while you are injured or ill for any reason. You may already have disability coverage if you work for a large company. You normally start receiving disability benefits three to six months after you become injured and unable to work.

Is disability insurance an important kind of insurance to have especially if I'm younger?

At age 25, you are much more likely to become disabled than you are to die. If you did become disabled, you would still need to pay for most of the things you pay for now, in addition to your new medical expenses. I'm not saying it is the *most* important insurance for you to have, but it is definitely up there.

What should I look for in a disability policy?

Most basically, you need to ask, if something happened and you needed to make a claim on this policy, what would you need to qualify for the benefits? In other words, how is disability defined in the policy you are interested in buying? Also, how long will you have to wait before benefits will be paid, and how long will they last?

Of course, every situation is different and you need to consider your own savings and other resources, but ideally you should have coverage that would pay you at least 60 to 70 percent of your income after an accident that leaves you unable to work at your current job. It should cover you in case of an illness or an accident, it should always be guaranteed renewable, and, in the best case, should offer a residual benefit protection (see below).

What is the most important element in a good disability policy?

What I would want to see in a policy is one that covered me for what is known as "owner's occupation," not "any occupation." An owner's occupation policy means that if I became disabled and could no longer perform my current occupation, the insurance company would have to pay me benefits. An any-occupation policy would only pay me if I could not perform any job at all. So for instance, let's say I am a writer and I need to be able to type, and for some reason I become disabled and am no longer able to do that. I would want the disability policy I had purchased to pay me benefits. However, if I had purchased an any-occupation disability policy, that policy would only pay me benefits if I could not even sell pencils on the corner, in other words, if I could not perform any occupation at all. Big difference.

Why is it so crucial that my disability insurance is guaranteed renewable?

Because your insurance company could cancel your policy if it isn't. This way, the only reason your policy could be cancelled would be if you stopped paying your premiums.

My agent suggested a modified-occupation disability policy. What does that mean?

This policy will pay you some benefit only if you can't work at a job that would be appropriate for someone of your age, education, and experience. Note that this might not mean the same job you had before, which means that you would still have to find employment if you are deemed capable of working at this level. For example, say you play the violin in your city's orchestra but you have an accident which seriously injures your hands. A modified-occupation disability policy would probably not pay out as long as you were still able to, for example, teach violin classes at a local college. Ask your agent to give you examples of what types of jobs you would be considered "qualified" for in a variety of different disabling circumstances. If the options would be unacceptable to you, you want to make sure that you have the owner's-only occupation coverage.

What if I can work at a new job, but it doesn't pay as well as the one I had when I became disabled?

This is when it is important to know that you have gotten the right kind of disability policy. You want your policy to have something called residual benefits. This means your policy will guarantee a certain percentage of your old job's income in comparison with your new job's income. For example, if your policy guarantees you a 75-percent residual benefit, and you became disabled, you would be guaranteed 75 percent of the income you made in your old job. If you were making $80,000 before your accident but your new, post-accident job only pays you $50,000, this residual benefit means that your insurance company will have to pay you $10,000 each year to make up the difference between your new salary ($50,000) and 75 percent of your old salary ($60,000).

What is the cheapest kind of disability policy?

The cheapest policies are normally those any-occupation policies which define disability as your inability to work any type of job at all. These have cheaper premiums because it is unlikely that you will ever become so thoroughly disabled that you cannot work at any job. Those small premiums aren't a bargain if the policy will only pay benefits if you are severely disabled.

I have been told to get a residual rider. Can you tell me what that means?

You can investigate getting additional benefits added to your disability coverage, such as residual benefit protection to have your insurance policy pay out a portion of your disability benefits in the event that you were partially disabled and only able to work part time, by adding what is called a residual rider to your policy. The problem with residual riders is that they tend to be expensive. If the coverage isn't already included in your policy, it may not be worth it. Your other resources and expenses will determine whether this is necessary.

How much will disability insurance cost me?

Your disability premiums will depend on your age, sex, job, and income, as well as the type of coverage you decide to purchase.

What kind of elimination period should disability insurance have?

The elimination period varies between policies. Try not to have more than a 60-day period between your injury (or the onset of your illness) and when your disability insurance kicks in. In the meantime, make sure that you are working toward establishing an emergency fund for yourself, if you have not already done so, so that you could cover the costs of living for a few months without your paycheck.

Would my disability benefits increase over time, if I am disabled forever?

You are right to ask about this, because if you were permanently disabled, it would become difficult to live on an income that doesn't keep pace with inflation. Cost of living adjustments or riders (COLA) cover this possibility and they may be included in your policy or they may cost extra. These riders allow you to increase your coverage (and your premiums, usually modestly) periodically without having an additional physical.

If I do not have disability insurance and something happens to me, will the state pay for me under state disability?

Yes, although this is not unlike an "any-occupation" disability policy—you generally have to be unable to work at any type of job. Please do not depend on the government to pay for you and your family if you become disabled. It is highly unlikely that, even if you qualified for these benefits, they would cover the expenses that you currently have.

My insurance agent is recommending that I purchase critical illness insurance because he says that it will fill the gaps between disability and life insurance. What do you think?

Critical care insurance policies specify a lot of different terrible things that could happen to you, such as a stroke or a heart attack, and, in exchange for your premiums, agree to give you one lump payment if you survive one of the qualifying illnesses or injuries. Your agent is probably suggesting that you would use that money to pay your medical expenses, but I'm telling you straight: *Please don't purchase this insurance.* While it is a type of term insurance, if you have extra money to spend on these premiums, you would be better off investing them yourself in a good no-load mutual fund or making sure that you have a good comprehensive health-care policy that will pay your major medical expenses no matter what kind of illness you have.

If something happens and I need to collect on my disability insurance, will I have to pay taxes on the benefits?
Many people have disability insurance through their job. If that's true for you, and your employer is paying your disability benefits, you will owe taxes. If you paid for your own disability insurance, then your benefits are not taxed.

How can I save money on my disability premiums?
As with other types of insurance policies, group coverage is often cheaper than buying an individual policy, so if you can tap into a group policy, it may be worthwhile. Also, think about how long you need the benefits to last and how long you could afford to wait before you began receiving disability benefits. If you have built an emergency savings fund of three to six months of your living expenses, you might be able to increase this exclusion period.

HOMEOWNER'S INSURANCE

If you financed your home when you purchased it, your lending institution required you to get some insurance on the building. But many people don't have enough coverage and they pay too much for what they do have. Your homeowner's insurance needs to cover the cost of rebuilding or repairing your house if it is damaged in a fire, a storm, a robbery, or other type of catastrophe. Below are the questions and answers that will help you decide if you have the right kind and right amount of insurance for your home.

What should a standard policy for my home cover?

Standard policies generally cover the contents of your house for half the amount that you insured the structure. In other words, if you insured your house for $150,000, your policy probably covers the contents of your home up to $75,000. Homeowner's policies also normally include liability coverage for damage incurred inside or outside your house, including if someone hurts themselves in your home.

What if the contents of my house are worth more than 50 percent of what my home is insured for?

You can increase your content coverage for a fee. Make sure that personal property insurance covers you for the replacement cost of your possessions, not their actual cash value. Figure out how much you need by making a list of everything you own and estimate what it would cost you to replace it all.

What are the basic types of homeowner's insurance I can buy?

There are six basic types of homeowner's insurance and there is renter's insurance:

- HO-1: This is a basic policy that protects your home from 14 named perils: fire, lightning, and external explosion; windstorms; hail; volcanic eruption; riot; civil commotion; vehicles; aircraft; smoke; vandalism and malicious mischief; glass breakage; and theft. As that's rarely enough, many states are phasing out this kind of coverage.

- HO-2: This is a broad policy that covers you against all the named perils included in HO-1 plus falling objects; the weight of ice, snow, or sleet; the collapse of buildings; accidental discharge or overflow of water or steam, or the explosion of steam or hot water systems; frozen plumbing, heating units, air conditioning systems, and domestic appliances; and power surges. People who have mobile homes are normally eligible for a variation of this type of policy.

- HO-3: This is a special policy that protects your home against all perils except for those that are explicitly excluded by the policy. Usually, the excluded perils are earthquakes, floods, termites, landslides, war, tidal waves, and nuclear accidents. This is the most common homeowner's policy.

  You can add an endorsement to an HO-3 that guarantees the replacement of your home and its contents, even if it exceeds your policy limit. Note that many companies do put a limit on this type of policy too, typically 120 or 150 percent of the face value of your policy.

- HO-4: This is renter's insurance. It normally protects the possessions of tenants in a house or apartment against the same perils specified in HO-3. It also provides some liability coverage but does not cover the actual dwelling, which it is the landlord's responsibility to insure. Make sure that your policy includes replacement cost coverage.

- HO-5: This is basically the same policy as HO-3 except it extends your coverage to your personal belongings. Sometimes, an insurance company won't sell HO-5 per se, and will instead sell you a rider to attach to HO-3.

- HO-6: This is a policy for co-op and condominium owners. Like HO-4, it provides coverage for liability and personal property. If you have made improvements to your particular unit (like a deck or built-in kitchen cabinets), you need to cover them under this policy type, rather than the policy that the co-op or condo association has for the actual dwelling. If you are in this situation, you might want to consider buying a "loss assessment" rider to protect you in case your co-op board or condo association needs to increase your maintenance or charges because of some uninsured loss to the building.

- HO-8: This is a type of policy that covers perils like those listed in HO-1, but is meant for people who own older homes, because it will insure the house only for repair costs or its actual cash value as opposed to its replacement cost, because to rebuild the home with the materials and details of the original would be prohibitively expensive. Basically, this policy will pay to restore the damaged property but not at the level of quality or authenticity of the original. This policy is rarely offered anymore.

Each homeowner's policy is divided into two sections. The first part covers your dwelling, other structures on the property, your personal property, and certain types of loss of use, like rental or additional living expenses. The other part should provide personal liability coverage, medical payments coverage, and additional coverage for claims expenses, first aid, and damage to other people's property.

Why would I need liability coverage in my homeowner's insurance?

This type of coverage is designed to protect your assets if you are sued by someone who is hurt or whose property is damaged due to your negligence. This could be damage you or a member of your family causes or even your pet (although certain types of attack dogs, such as pit bulls and the like, will be excluded from your policy). An example would be if you lived in a two-family house, and you turned the water on to run yourself a bath but then took a phone call. You forgot about your tub, and it overflowed and damaged the ceiling of the unit below you. Liability coverage should pay to repair that damage.

What is the difference between an actual cash value policy and a replacement cost policy?

An actual cash value policy will reimburse you for the cost of your belongings less their depreciation, while a replacement cost policy means that the insurance company must reimburse you for the actual cost of replacing the lost or damaged item. If you have a couch that you purchased for $1,000 a few years ago, a cash value policy might only reimburse you for $800 for that couch, assuming a depreciation of 20 percent, while a replacement cost policy would pay you to get the exact same couch. You can see why replacement cost policies are better.

What does the medical payments section cover if I already have comprehensive medical coverage?

Again, your comprehensive health insurance should pay for you no matter what. This coverage is for protection in the event that *someone else* injures themselves on your property or because of your negligence and needs medical care. The classic example might be your mail carrier falling and injuring his back because your walkway was covered with ice and snow which you failed to remove.

Will homeowner's insurance cover all my personal property?

Commonly restricted items on a homeowner's insurance policy include specifically insured items such as jewelry, furs, or cameras (for which you can get primary coverage elsewhere), and any pets you have, including birds or fish (although separate policies are available for them). Vehicle coverage is generally excluded, as is coverage for electronic equipment, like a radio, in your vehicles. You probably won't be covered for property that may belong to someone other than your relatives, business-related items, or credit card losses.

I rent one of my extra bedrooms to a college student. Would my homeowner's policy cover her property if my home were broken into?

Usually not, because most policies only cover your property (as the policyholder) and the property of people related to you who live in your house.

So if I have $200,000 in homeowner's insurance and my house is destroyed, do I get $200,000?

Not necessarily. In many policies you actually have to rebuild the property for you to get this money. Limits often apply to the cost of rebuilding the structure of your home.

Does my homeowner's insurance cover damage to my garage?

Separate structures on your property—a garage, a shed, or a guest house—sometimes need to be covered separately. If your garage is attached to your house, it is part of the total dwelling cost. Your landscaping, if you have a lot invested in your trees and shrubs, may also need to be covered separately. Check your policy carefully to see if such items are covered.

What should I do if something terrible happens and I need to make a claim?

Your insurance company will either send you a "proof of loss" form to complete or will arrange for an adjuster to visit your house. Either way, you need to document your loss as best you can to make sure that you get the full value that you are entitled to under the policy.

What is the best way of documenting my losses?

Make a list of everything that was stolen or damaged, and provide a description of each item, the date you bought it, and, if you have replacement-cost coverage, what it would cost to replace it. If you have receipts, bills, photographs, or serial numbers, these things will generally help your case. Hold onto your damaged items until the adjuster has a chance to look at them. Take photographs or videos of any damage to your house, noting everything you want the adjuster to see, from cracks in the walls to missing tiles. Generally, you have one year to amend your claim if you find additional damage. It can be helpful, if tedious, to prepare for this possibility ahead of time, by videotaping the contents and condition of your home, and keeping records on the details of your major purchases.

You said jewelry might be restricted, and I found out that in fact it is in my policy. My insurance company will only pay up to $1,000 for all jewelry, and I know my

engagement ring alone is worth more than that. How can I increase this protection?

Many policies limit the amount of money your insurance company would pay for specific items such as jewelry or computer equipment. If the standard coverage is too low for your comfort, you can buy additional protection by adding an amendment called an endorsement to protect a particular item (like your engagement ring). But please make sure that it's really worth paying the extra premiums to extend your coverage on the items.

What is off-premise protection?

Many homeowner's policies cover your possessions outside your house. For example, if you are mugged on the street or your luggage is stolen on vacation, off-premise protection should reimburse you for the items you lose. If you need to pay extra for this coverage, think carefully about the size of the deductible and the likelihood that you would be carrying around items that are worth more. If the deductible is pretty high, and you don't normally run around wearing or carrying a lot of expensive stuff, it might not be worth it. And be careful if the big-ticket items you do tend to travel with are things like your engagement ring or your laptop computer. If they are only covered up to a certain level and you haven't extended their protection, a high deductible on top of the reimbursement restriction could make this coverage a waste of time.

What is loss of use protection?

Most policies include some protection in case you can't use your home because it's been damaged or while it's being repaired. This should reimburse you for the cost of modest motel bills and meals while repairs are underway. Up to 30 percent of your home's value is not an unusual maximum for this type of coverage.

My bank required me to get a certain level of home-owner's insurance, so that's what I got. If it weren't enough, wouldn't they have made me purchase more? If your coverage isn't enough to cover the bank's expenses, yes, they probably would require you to buy more coverage. But the bank is not concerned about whether your expenses would be covered, particularly for your personal property. Don't assume that the bank is looking out for you.

What is a standard level of coverage for things other than my house, and how do I determine how much coverage I need? Usually your personal property is insured at 50 percent of the value of your home and you can increase the amount of coverage by paying higher premiums. Other buildings on your property, like your garage or a shed, are normally insured at 10 percent of your home's value, while your trees and other landscape elements are covered at 5 percent. In other words, if your home was insured for $100,000, a standard policy would cover your personal property for $50,000, your free-standing garage at $10,000, and your shrubs for $5,000. You need to find out what your policy will cover and decide whether these figures would be enough to replace or restore everything.

Bottom line, financially, what should I look for in homeowner's insurance? You want to be able to replace your home and its contents if something should happen to your house. The cost of doing that after a catastrophic loss will probably be greater than the depreciated cash value of your property. This means that, as usual, you want replacement cost coverage. You also want to have automatic inflation adjustments built into your policy.

MORTGAGE PROTECTION INSURANCE

What is the difference between private mortgage insurance and mortgage protection insurance?

If you bought your home without putting down at least 20 percent of its cost, you probably had to buy private mortgage insurance (PMI) to get your mortgage and you probably had to pay it until you had at least 20 percent equity in your home. It protected the lender in case you stopped making your mortgage payments and the house went into foreclosure. (See *Ask Suze . . . About Real Estate* to learn more about PMI.) Some insurance agencies will offer to sell you mortgage protection insurance, which is basically an arrangement where you pay your premiums and, should you die before your mortgage is paid and while your policy is still in effect, the insurance company pays off whatever is left on your mortgage.

Do the premiums on mortgage protection insurance go down as the balance on my mortgage goes down?

No. Your premiums will stay the same, because they are calculated with that decrease in mind.

What if I send my mortgage payments in ahead of time?

Then the policy should pay your beneficiaries what the amount of your mortgage should have been at the time of your death, had you only been sending in checks according to the payment schedule. The extra money, after the mortgage is paid off, would belong to your beneficiaries.

How do I know if I need mortgage protection insurance?
Most likely you do not, though of course you need to consider your individual situation. Do you have beneficiaries who will need a place to live without worrying about making mortgage payments? Still, in that case, I really think that it would make more sense to buy a good term life insurance policy that would include enough money to pay off your mortgage as well as provide for other needs your family might have after you are gone.

We just refinanced our mortgage. What happens to our old mortgage protection insurance?
If you still want to keep it, call your insurance company because you will probably be able to get a new policy with a lower premium.

Is there any way to reduce my premiums on mortgage protection insurance?
Some companies do offer a modest reduction if you and your spouse both have this type of coverage. But if you have made the decision to protect your home this way instead of just covering this cost on your term life insurance policy, consider whether you both really need it. If you both contribute equally to paying your mortgage, then maybe it makes sense, but if one of you does not work outside the home, for example, it doesn't make sense for you to both have this coverage, since, presumably, your working spouse will be able to continue working and making these payments after you are gone.

I work from home and have expensive computer equipment that is worth a lot more than my personal property coverage would reimburse me for. What happens if it's damaged or stolen?

This is very common. You need to buy a "floater" that will increase your coverage for particular items, but it will cost you additional money, so make sure you're assessing the value of those items realistically. If you have a home office and are using your computer equipment for business or professional reasons, you may need to purchase additional coverage as well. Ask your insurance agent what type of coverage is available under those circumstances.

If I am going on a trip for more than a month, do I need to notify the insurance company?

Every policy is different, so you should check yours to see if it has this type of requirement, because if it does and you fail to follow it and need to make a claim, your insurance company could refuse to pay your claim. Many insurance companies don't require this if you are going to be away from your primary residence for a month or two but absolutely require notification if you have another property, say, that you rent, and it is going to be vacant for a month or more.

My brother and I are doing some work on my house but haven't bothered getting a permit. If something happened, like a fire, would my homeowner's policy still be valid?

I'm glad you asked this question, because if the work that you're doing causes a fire and you don't have a permit, you will not be covered. You could probably get in a dispute with your insurance company if the fire starts because of something unrelated to the illegal work, but that could take a long time to resolve and the outcome is not guaranteed. In short, get the permit.

You keep mentioning that increasing my deductible will reduce my premium costs. Can you be more specific about what that means in terms of homeowner's insurance?

The Insurance Information Institute estimates that if you started with a $250 deductible and raised it to $500, your premiums should be reduced by as much as 12 percent. If you increased your deductible to $1,000, your premiums should be reduced by up to 24 percent. If you increased to a $2,500 deductible, your premiums could be up to 30 percent lower. Remember, you are taking a gamble that you will save more on your premiums that you will ultimately wind up paying in deductibles. Just be sure that you will actually be able to pay the deductible if you need to.

How can I save on homeowner's insurance?

If you can afford it, raise your deductible. Buy your homeowner's and car insurance from the same company, as long as both policies compare favorably to others you're considering. Take steps to make your home safe: Buy fire extinguishers, install smoke detectors, security systems, and deadbolt locks. And this is yet another good reason not to smoke. Ask your insurance agent about these measures; you may find that they all translate into cost reductions. Ask about senior citizen reductions, loyal customer reductions if you have been with your insurance company for at least five years, and investigate whether any associations you belong to offer discounted group coverage. Finally, here's a common mistake: Don't include the value of your land when you are figuring out how much insurance to purchase. Your lot isn't included in the coverage, so it doesn't make sense to pay as though it were.

RENTER'S INSURANCE

I don't own a home yet, I only rent. Do I need renter's insurance?

If you have personal property damaged by a fire or you were robbed, how much would it cost you to replace what you own? It doesn't matter whether the home your possessions are in belongs to you or someone else, right? Many renter's insurance policies also contain some liability protection for you as well, in case you damage your apartment or in case someone else is hurt in your apartment. If you have anything of value that you want to protect then, in my opinion, renter's insurance is a good thing.

Does renter's insurance just cover my personal property?

Actually, no. Usually there is liability and medical payments coverage, if someone injures themselves in your apartment and sues you along with the landlord. Also, renter's insurance can cover your loss of use if something catastrophic should happen to the building and you were forced to live somewhere else while the owners repair or rebuild it. This can be key protection for renters, since you often don't have as much control over the maintenance of your property and its systems as owners do.

UMBRELLA LIABILITY POLICIES

This is a special type of policy that may be right for you if you have a lot of assets, or the potential to accumulate a lot of assets. It offers additional personal liability protection beyond your homeowner's or car liability coverage and may protect you if you're sued for something not covered by other insurance, such as libel, slander, wrongful eviction, or false arrest. Umbrella policies may be a better deal than increasing your liability coverage separately under each of your additional policies.

Why would I purchase liability insurance or what is known as an umbrella policy?

If your assets are worth a lot more than the liability limits of your homeowner's policy, it may make sense to investigate an umbrella policy. It will start paying after your regular policy has reached its limit.

But if I increase my liability coverage, won't that just give someone who sues me that much more money?

That's why it is important if you already have a significant amount of assets that you need to protect, so that someone can't sue you for those instead.

How do I know if I need an umbrella liability policy?

Assuming that you don't have a special concern about being sued for something like wrongful eviction, look at the limits of your other liability coverages and figure out if they seem adequate relative to your other assets. If they aren't, you should compare the cost of purchasing an umbrella liability policy with the cost of increasing the limits on your other policies.

FLOOD INSURANCE

I am about to buy a home in what they call a low- to medium-risk area for floods. Do I need flood insurance?

I have to tell you, more and more I think you do. Between 20 and 25 percent of the flood insurance claims come from low- to medium-risk areas. The pictures of the devastation Hurricane Floyd inflicted on the East Coast in 1999 were shocking—all the more so because many of those areas had never experienced a flood before.

If I do not have flood insurance, is there a national program that will help me in case of a natural disaster?

Yes, if your area is declared a federal disaster area, then you can get help through the Federal Emergency Management Agency (FEMA) from the crippling financial losses often caused by flooding.

If FEMA will give me money to replace my home, why should I pay for private flood insurance?

Because often floods are too small or too localized to qualify for federal assistance. Even if a flood does qualify, the assistance from FEMA comes as grants or loans. Grants are usually given in amounts that barely cover losses, much less enable you to rebuild. And disaster home loans, with an average repayment plan of 18.5 years, must be repaid with interest on top of your existing mortgage payment.

The bottom line is that there is a big difference between paying back a loan, even if it is at a low interest rate, and having an insurance plan that will pay for everything.

How much does a flood insurance policy cost?

The average flood insurance premium costs a little over $300 a year for an average of $100,000 of coverage. Please note that if you were to take out a FEMA loan of just $50,000 to help you replace your articles lost in a flood, that loan would cost you an average of $300 a month for an average repayment period of close to 20 years!

Does FEMA offer flood insurance?

Yes. Under FEMA's National Flood Insurance Program (NFIP), federally backed flood insurance is available in communities that adopt and enforce regulations to reduce flood losses. Remember, flood insurance provides coverage that your homeowner's insurance doesn't—coverage for damages caused by floods. The good news is that nearly 19,000 communities in the United States and its territories that are faced with potential flooding participate in the NFIP, so the chances are excellent that NFIP insurance is available to you.

For more information about NFIP flood insurance and if it is available in your particular area, call the NFIP at 1-888-CALL-FLOOD, ext. 445. Believe it or not, you will get a live person on the phone (as of the writing of this book) who can answer your questions.

I am about to buy a home in a high-risk flood area and my mortgage broker is telling me that I have to buy flood insurance. Is this correct?

Yes, if you are buying a house in a designated high-risk area, and receive a mortgage loan from a federally regulated lender, your lender must, by law, require that you buy flood insurance.

What is the maximum flood insurance I can buy?

- Up to $250,000 for single-family, two-to-four family, and other residential buildings;
- Up to $500,000 for nonresidential buildings, including small businesses;
- Up to $100,000 for contents coverage for residences for owners and/or renters;
- Up to $500,000 for contents for businesses, including small businesses.

If I am a renter in a high-risk flood area, can I buy flood insurance?

Yes.

If I hear on the news that a flooding is expected in my area, can I get a policy right away?

No. Policies go into effect 30 days after a policy is purchased. So please do not wait until you are faced with that emergency to get yourself covered.

If I own my home outright and I live in a high flood area am I still required to buy flood insurance?

If you own your house outright, no federal agency will force you to buy flood insurance or keep the flood insurance you had to have when you still had a mortgage. Property owners who do not have a mortgage insured by a federal agency are free to buy the insurance or not buy the insurance—it all depends on your assessment of the risk that you will be taking.

EARTHQUAKE INSURANCE

Many of us trust that after a natural disaster, the government will step in with aid so that any financial losses we suffer will eventually be recouped. That is not generally true. The government is likely to provide disaster assistance, but it does not protect the individual homeowner from loss. The most common federal aid after a disaster comes in the form of low-interest loans, which must be paid back over time.

Earthquakes, like floods, are disasters that inflict massive and widespread damage on a region all at once. This introduces logistical difficulties for insurance companies, who may need to cover enormous claims all at once. With fire, auto, and life insurance claims, the losses are smaller and more frequent, and the statistics are thoroughly understood.

In the last decade, the insurance industry has paid out record amounts of money for insured losses caused by earthquakes and hurricanes. Because of this, the insurance industry has come up with two main ways to deal with the possibilities of large losses due to earthquakes. The first is that some insurers are choosing not to accept new policies or renewals in areas of high seismic risk. The other way is that insurers have been working with Congress to establish a federal natural disaster insurance program to augment the capacity of private industry to provide disaster insurance. If you live in an area that is prone to earthquakes, you should be aware of the following facts about earthquake insurance. Please note: While the principles of earthquake insurance are the same in every state, the specifics about coverage, availability, and affordability vary from company to company and state to state.

Who sells earthquake insurance?

In general, only large multi-line, multi-state companies insure catastrophes. Only a few companies sell earthquake insurance. Even in California, which is the most earthquake-prone of all our states, only about 175 insurers actively sell earthquake insurance, out of a total of about 800 property/casualty insurers and about 700 life and health insurers.

There could be some type of federal involvement in the provision of earthquake insurance if Congress passes legislation creating a federally-backed insurance program, but as of the writing of this book that has not yet happened, though a new state-managed program has just been initiated in California.

I have been offered earthquake insurance from a small insurance company and the rates are far better than those I've been offered by a large company. Which way should I go?

Watch out. Small insurance companies usually lack the financial resources to pay for a large catastrophic event. Better to stay away from small insurers offering earthquake coverage.

What does a typical earthquake insurance policy cover?

A typical earthquake policy insures for loss against structural damage, damage to contents, and loss of use (residential) or business income (commercial).

What does loss of use coverage or business income mean?

Loss of use covers the costs of a hotel or other rental and meals until the structure is repaired. Business income covers the income and rental losses arising from the shutdown of the business (sometimes called business interruption).

Everyone tells me that earthquake insurance is not worth it because of the high deductible. Do you agree?
It is true that earthquake insurance policies have high deductibles. A typical deductible is 10 percent to 15 percent of the value of your property. So if your home is worth $200,000 and your deductible is 10 percent, then you would be responsible for the first 10 percent or $20,000 worth of damage to that home before your policy would kick in. The same would be true for your contents. The reason that many people say it is not worth it is that for a well-built wood-frame house, this deductible generally exceeds the structural loss for most moderate earthquakes. Due to improvements in structural soundness and design, recent earthquakes have caused less damage to structures than to the contents within those structures.

I live in California and was just offered a policy by the CEA. What is the CEA?
Pressure put on state officials by insurance carriers to carry earthquake insurance has resulted in the creation of the California Earthquake Authority (CEA). This new agency provides "mini" earthquake insurance policies, not covering pools, patios, fences, driveways, or detached garages. The deductible will be 15 percent. These policies cover no more than $5,000 worth of a home's contents and provide a maximum of $1,500 in living expenses.

The rating plan approved by CEA has a statewide average rate of $3.29 for every $1,000 of coverage, with homeowners in low-risk areas paying less and those in high-risk areas paying more. So for instance, the cost is highest in San Francisco, where the policy for a $300,000 wood-frame house built before 1960 would cost $1,710 per year. In Sacramento, the same policy would cost $600. If an earthquake produces more claims than available resources can handle and you have a CEA policy, you may be required to pay an assessment which could add up to as much as 20 percent of future earthquake premiums, The cost of these new policies varies throughout the state, depending on the earthquake risk and the age and construction of the home.

What questions should I ask an agent when buying an earthquake policy?

- Why should I buy earthquake insurance?
- Is there another way for me to replace my property if I don't have earthquake insurance?
- Is the earthquake insurance coverage included in my existing homeowner's policy or do I have to buy a separate policy?
- What will earthquake insurance cover?
- How much earthquake insurance coverage should I buy?
- How much will it cost me annually?
- Will the coverage I buy apply to the combined value of my house (the structure itself) and the contents of my home (furniture, clothing, electronic equipment, collections, etc.), or should I evaluate my potential losses separately?
- How much is the deductible?
- Is the deductible for my earthquake insurance coverage different from the deductible for my basic homeowner's coverage?

- How is the deductible on my earthquake insurance coverage going to be calculated in the event of a loss? Will a separate deductible apply to the structure, contents, and detached structures, or does one deductible apply to the entire loss?

- Does the policy have a guaranteed replacement cost coverage? If so, how would this coverage apply if I suffered a loss?

- If you own a condominium, ask how earthquake insurance would benefit you. (Ask specifically what insurance would cover if you were forced to vacate the premises for safety reasons.)

- If you're a renter, ask how earthquake insurance would benefit you. (Ask specifically if additional living expenses would be covered if you were forced to vacate the premises for safety reasons.)

- Will my car be covered by earthquake insurance?

- What about other structures—the garage, for instance? Would it be covered by the same policy or will I need to get a separate policy or add a rider to my primary policy?

- If I have to vacate my home, will earthquake insurance cover the hotel expenses? If so, for how long?

- Is breakage of fragile articles covered if I purchase earthquake insurance? Is there a better way to cover these items?

- Does the type of home I live in (brick, veneer, masonry) affect the way earthquake coverage will respond?

- Does the earthquake policy exclude certain repairs?

- How long do I have to wait after an earthquake before I can file a claim?

- What about aftershocks attributable to the original quake—would I be covered for resulting damages without another deductible?
- Are there additional "endorsements" to the earthquake coverage that I should also consider, such as building code upgrades, structural report coverage, demolition, etc.?

LIFE INSURANCE

Life insurance was never meant to be a permanent need. Its original purpose was to protect people while they were younger, before they had a chance to build up a nest egg, in case the family breadwinner died early and unexpectedly. If the breadwinner lived his or her life according to plan, however, the family would accumulate enough assets to secure itself and then let the insurance go.

Today, however, a huge industry exists to sell you as much insurance as it can, whether you really need it or not.

I know how the industry works, because I'm a licensed insurance agent, and even though selling life insurance is not my favorite thing, I know the workings of most policies inside out. I also know how the commissions work. If you knew how large those commissions really are—often 80 to 90 percent of the first year's premium—you would know why people say that life insurance isn't something you buy. Life insurance is something that's sold to you.

If you're single and have no dependents at all, you can skip this section, because there is no need for you to have life insurance. However, if you have people who depend on the money you bring in with every paycheck, there is information here that is essential for you to understand.

These are the four basic questions to ask yourself about life insurance:

- Do I need it?
- How much do I need?
- How long will I need it?
- What kind of life insurance policy do I need?

How do I know if I need life insurance?

You need to compile a list of all your expenses and compare them to how much income you actually have coming in. In other words, you need to sort out how much you truly spend each and every month. After you have done that, you need to review those expenses and see how drastically your financial situation would change if your children were suddenly parentless or if you or your partner were to die. Fixed expenses, like your mortgage payment, would remain the same. Some expenses, maybe the grocery bill, would decrease. Some expenses would increase—long-distance phone calls to friends for comfort, eating out so you wouldn't be so lonely, entertainment. Would your child-care situation change? What about the future financial goals you had—paying for your children's education, for example? Could you still cover that? What if you or your partner had to stop working as well? How would you cope? How much would it really take? How much do you have saved?

Now compare the hypothetical money coming in against the hypothetical money going out in this scenario and any other scenarios you can imagine. What impact would a possible death have on the money coming in? If your survivors would have enough, then you do not need insurance. You may still want some for your emotional peace of mind, but you don't *need* it—and there is a big difference between *needing* insurance and *wanting* it.

If they would not have enough, then you know you need insurance to protect yourself and your loved ones.

How much life insurance do I need?

Most people think all they'd need is enough to get their family by until they come to terms with the loss. As a result, they usually have the $50,000 or so worth of insurance that's part of their benefits package at work and think that this will be sufficient. But since an unexpected tragedy affects people in different ways, you never know for sure what might happen after you are gone. That's why this is a decision that must be discussed with the people who would be affected by such an event, taking into account every tragic possibility. All the questions must be asked: Would they feel comfortable knowing that they have enough money to get by for a year, or two, or eight?

My insurance agent says I don't need to go through all this, that I can just buy enough coverage to replace my salary for eight years. Is that wrong?

Many experts will tell you to purchase six to eight times your annual salary, but experts are not the ones who have to live your loved ones' lives. Maybe in your situation you would rather know that everyone will be okay no matter what, even if no one is ever able to work again. Maybe you want to provide for your children for ten years, rather than just eight. There is no magic formula. Each of us has our own financial what-if comfort level. The final decision is a balance of what makes everyone concerned feel secure and how much you can realistically afford to pay for that security.

Is there any kind of financial guideline you can give me?
As a rule of thumb, I would figure that you need about
$100,000 in insurance for every $500 of monthly income required. Let's say your household needs $3,000 a month to
cover all expenses. Your worst-case scenario is that the people
who survive you have no employment or other income, so
they'll need the full $3,000. You'd divide this by $500 and get
six, so your insurance policy should be in the amount of six
times $100,000, or $600,000.

What's the theory behind that recommendation?
This is the idea: You want your insurance payment to be a sum
of money that your beneficiaries can invest to generate enough
income to cover their expenses without having to dip into the
principal. If their monthly expenses would be $3,000, that's
$36,000 a year. Assuming a conservative interest rate of 6 per-
cent, you would need $600,000 to produce that $36,000 a
year. That principal would go on throwing off income forever
because your survivors are using only the interest.

***In my case, if I die, I know that my wife would need to
have some support, but she makes the same amount of
money that I do and I know she would continue to work
after I died. How do I figure out what she would need?***
Assuming you also have monthly expenses of $3,000, all she
would need from the insurance proceeds, before taxes, is
$1,500 a month. You have three choices. You can purchase the
minimum amount of insurance needed to cover that shortage
of $1,500 a month, which is $300,000 worth of insurance
($1,500 divided by 500 is three; three times $100,000 is
$300,000). Or you can purchase $600,000 worth of insurance
to cover yourself completely, in case at some later date she won't

be able to work after all. Or you can purchase any amount in between that would make you both feel comfortable.

If I go ahead and buy that $600,000 coverage, just to be on the safe side, and something happened to me and then all my wife needed was $1,500 a month from the death benefit to cover her expenses, what should she do with the $600,000?

She will want to invest enough safely for the principal to generate that $1,500 a month in interest every year, without touching the principal, and invest the rest for growth in case the day comes when she can't work anymore or she loses her job. Let's figure again. How much needs to be invested for income, to cover the $1,500 a month she needs, and how much for growth? To find out how much she needs to invest in order to generate $1,500 a month before taxes, multiply $1,500 by 12 to find out how much she needs per year—$18,000. Let's assume that the going interest rate is 6 percent (a conservative figure, but to be safe, it's always best to think conservatively). So how much does she need to invest at 6 percent to generate $18,000 a year? We divide 100 (percent of any whole) by six (the interest rate we're after), which gives us almost exactly 17. Now we multiply $18,000 by 17 to see how much needs to be invested at 6 percent to generate $18,000 a year: $306,000 ($306,000 times 6 percent equals $18,360). She received a total of $600,000 in insurance proceeds, and now she knows that she has to invest $306,000 for income generation for as long as she continues to bring home the $1,500 monthly paycheck. The remaining $294,000 is what she can invest for growth—and also serves as backup if something should happen to her. You have covered all your bases. If you had decided simply to purchase the minimum amount of insurance needed in this situation, which was $300,000, she would have to invest all of that to generate the $1,500 a month income she needed and hope she was able to keep on working while she built up more of a nest egg.

I did everything you said and I talked to my partner, and the bottom line is, we just can't afford to buy as much insurance as I would like. Any suggestions?
With my clients there's almost always a discrepancy between the maximum of insurance wanted and the minimum of insurance needed. Your needs, comfort level, and what you can afford all have to be taken into account. If you're using a professional to help you figure this out, make sure he or she has your needs and pocketbook in mind and isn't just thinking of all that the commissions will buy. I would suggest that you're better off trying to figure out how much insurance you really need and can afford, then calling to get quotes to compare the best-priced policies.

Are there any quote services that you particularly recommend?
Make sure that you check with at least three of the following services; you would be surprised how much they can differ:

Insurance Quote Services (800) 972-1104
Term-quote (800) 444-8376
Master Quote of America (800) 337-5433
Liferates (800) 457-2837
Quote Smith (800) 431-1147
Select Quote (800) 343-1985

How long will I need to keep my life insurance policy?

Remember, life insurance was never intended to be an ongoing need. As the years go by, the money that you put away in your retirement plan, the money you may accumulate on your own, and the mortgage you're paying off so that you'll own your own house outright are all factors that will continue to change how much insurance you really need or whether you need it at all. One of your goals should be to make sure that by the time you are retired, you'll have enough coming in from your retirement plans to support yourself, and your loved ones after you're gone. Once you have enough to live on in this way, most likely there will be no need for life insurance. That said, never, *never* cancel or attempt to change a policy without checking with your doctor and having a thorough physical. If there's a medical reason, you may want to keep insurance you otherwise would not have needed. Bottom-line goal: By the time you are 65 at the latest, your need for life insurance, and your need to pay the premiums on your life insurance, should be gone.

What should I replace my coverage with?

There are many possibilities: investments and pension plans, to name but two. If you look in *Ask Suze . . . About Planning for Your Future* and the books in this series about investments, you can read in more detail about how you can set up a financial plan to meet your goals. Once you figure out how long it's going to take you to save for that level of protection, you'll know how long you need your life insurance policy.

What kind of life insurance do I need?

In my opinion, there is only one kind of life insurance that makes sense for the vast majority of us, and that is term life insurance. When you sign up for term insurance, you're buying a just-in-case policy for a finite length of time that you need protection. These policies are not very expensive, because the insurance company knows you have relatively little chance of dying while the policy is in force. Most likely they won't have to pay a death benefit, and the premium is, accordingly, relatively small.

What is the difference between term life insurance and a cash value policy, also known as whole life insurance?

Term life insurance protects you for a certain number of years (typically one to 20), and once the "term" of the policy is over, you can usually renew it and begin another term without providing evidence of insurability each time, though often at a higher cost. If you die during the term of the policy, the insurance company pays out a specific amount of money to your beneficiaries. This is the death benefit. Because you do not build any cash value and it is protection only for a specific length of time, it follows that when you are younger, term life insurance is the least expensive kind of life insurance. However, the older you get, the more expensive term insurance becomes, because it is more likely that the company will have to pay out the death benefit. By the time you are in your 70s, the premiums on term life insurance will be very high, but, if you have planned properly, you should no longer need it.

A cash value policy is a "permanent" policy or what is known to most of you as a whole life policy, in which you are guaranteed coverage. Your premiums are priced accordingly, since the insurance companies know that they are probably going to have to pay out the death benefit since you intend to have it for the rest of your life and not just for a term of time. These policies have a cash value, which means that the insurance company takes your annual premium, deducts some administrative fees, the cost of death protection, and a profit margin and puts the rest (your "cash value") into a type of savings account.

Which is better, term or whole life insurance?

Term life insurance is the most cost-effective insurance you can buy. There is really no comparison. Term life insurance policies are cheap. Why? Because people are living longer, so insurance companies don't have to pay out as many life insurance claims. This is key to understanding life insurance: Insurance companies sell insurance to make money. They are selling you a term life insurance policy at a reasonable rate when you are young because they know that it is unlikely that you are going to die during the term. You are buying life insurance, I hope, because you want to know that the people who depend on you will be taken care of if you die and you haven't saved enough money yet to feel secure about that. You want a flexible, inexpensive policy that will give you that security without costing you very much, because you probably won't need it. Whole life insurance is mostly just an expensive way to save money.

Are there different types of term life insurance policies?

Yes. You can buy what is known as a level term policy for a number of years. This is where your premiums would be level for the length of time you have chosen, usually 5, 10, 15, or 20 years. The insurance company takes your current age into consideration and the term of the policy you are buying and figures out the average stable premium you will have to pay to keep the policy in effect for all those years. Obviously, the older you are and the longer the term you sign up for, the higher the premium will be.

You can also buy annual guaranteed-renewable term insurance, where at the end of each year if you still need the policy, you can renew it, though the premiums will be increased to reflect your new age.

Another option is decreasing term insurance (which is normally considered by people whose main financial obligation also decreases, like a mortgage) that starts with a specific death benefit that decreases each year until your policy expires at zero.

The last kind of term insurance is not as commonly needed or sold, but you may come across a type of increasing term life insurance, which provides a death benefit that rises steadily as the term continues.

If I get term life insurance, what size term should I look for?

The longest period of coverage that you can purchase is usually no more than 20 or 30 years and many people will tell you to buy the longest term you can in order to lock in a relatively low rate. I recommend buying a term that will last long enough for you to save money to take care of your family on your own, through your own investments and savings.

My insurance agent had policies that had other names besides whole and term. Are there different types of cash value accounts?

Yes. The most common types are whole life, universal life, and variable life. Whole life and universal life policies mean that the insurance company will invest your cash value and give you a specific interest rate. Variable life policies give you mutual-fund type options for your cash value and you can choose how to invest those funds.

So does my death benefit grow as my cash value accumulates?

Yes and no. That is a decision you can make when you purchase this type of insurance. Your death benefit is constant, which means it is paid out at the same rate at any time that the policy is in effect. Your premiums are also constant in cash value policies, and are designed to remain the same until the policy matures at age 100 (the age when your premium payments would cease and the cash value would equal the face amount). Most people, obviously, do not expect to live to age 100.

My insurance agent told me that cash value life insurance is better because it offers tax-favored growth. Is that true?

Yes and no. Money that you invest in a cash value life insurance policy will grow tax deferred—if and when it grows. Remember that the commissions on most cash value policies are high, sometimes more than 100 percent of your first year's premium. It is not uncommon for a whole life policy to lose money in its first five or six years, partially because of the commissions and administrative fees. This may explain why your insurance agent is so enthusiastic about this type of policy. There are many other ways to invest and save money on taxes without paying a commission or lots of fees: Put your money in an IRA or a 401(k) and you'll find a similar tax benefit and, the odds are, more growth.

What is universal life insurance?

This is a variation of whole life insurance, except that the investment portion of your insurance premiums goes into money market funds and grows at a variable rate. After your first payment, this type of policy allows you to pay premiums at any time and in any amount within a particular minimum and maximum rate set in the contract. The premiums you pay and the interest that your money earns is the amount of cash value that your policy has at any given time, less the expenses of the insurance company, which can be considerable and can also increase over time. As with whole life insurance, the insurance company will be making many of the investment decisions.

It's true that whole life and universal policies have cash values, so if you decide not to keep it, or if you suddenly need money while you're alive, one source would be the cash value of these policies. But commissions on life insurance policies are some of the most lucrative commissions in any business— and you're paying them. If your goal in buying life insurance is to put money aside, there are far, far better ways to save it without having to pay these kinds of commissions.

What is variable life insurance?

Also similar to whole life insurance, this type of policy provides death benefits or cash values that vary according to the investment returns of stock and bond funds managed by your insurance company (although you can choose where to invest your premiums). This can be a very uncertain type of policy because your premiums change and there is no guaranteed cash value, although it can theoretically also pay off at higher rates than whole or universal life policies. Remember, though, that the risk is to your money.

Can I borrow money against a whole life insurance policy?

You can take out what is called a policy loan against your policy as long as it isn't for more than the cash value your policy will have on its next anniversary. In many cases you don't ever have to repay this loan, for the amount of money that is left in the policy generates enough interest to pay the loan charges, but if you don't, the death benefit that gets paid out will be less the amount of your loan plus interest. The interest rate that you have to pay for a loan would be set in your contract.

I realize that you don't recommend it, but if I wanted, could I convert a term policy into a whole life policy?
Yes, many term policies are "convertible," which means they can be exchanged for another type of policy, including whole life. Frequently, that would involve paying the difference between the premiums for the two policies. But in most cases, I'd advise you never to do this. If you are unhappy with your term insurance for some reason, look for a different term policy that would better meet your needs. Make sure that your new policy is in force before you drop your old one.

Okay, I made the big mistake and bought a whole life policy. What should I do with it now?
First, you need to go to a doctor and make sure that he or she gives you a clean bill of health. Then, once you know you are healthy, you can apply for and purchase a term life insurance policy for however long you think it's going to take you to save and invest enough money to provide for your family on your own. Once you have been approved for your new term policy, then and only then can you cash out your whole life policy and invest the "cash value" in a good no-load mutual fund. Add to your investment with the difference you are saving in your premiums, which will be much cheaper now.

I told my insurance agent that I want to cash out my whole life policy but he says I'm crazy because it's only over the long run that these policies make money. He says if I take it out now I'll be losing money. Is that true?

You may be losing some of your investment in the short term because the insurance company has deducted so many fees, but you are almost certainly going to make it up and then some over the long run (10 or more years) if you invest that cash value and the excess premium money into a no-load mutual fund. The insurance company is the party that is really going to lose money, because they won't have the use of yours anymore.

Will I have to pay taxes if I cash my whole life insurance policy out?

If you cancel the policy, you get a lump sum payout and you will pay taxes on it only if the cash value plus your dividends equal more than the total of all the premiums that you paid into it—frequently, it won't be, which is why you are cashing this out in the first place.

What happens if I stop paying my premiums on a whole life insurance policy?

Usually you have a certain amount of time (often a few years) to reinstate, or renew the policy as long as you can establish your insurability again. If you find yourself in this situation, don't just automatically get your old policy reinstated. Make sure that it is still better than any new policy that you could get.

What is double indemnity?

Many life insurance policies pay double the death benefit if the death of the insured is accidental. For instance, if your death happened because of a car accident, and you had this feature on a $200,000 policy, it would pay out at $400,000. Something like a heart attack would not count. It should be noted, however, that this benefit is paid very infrequently. For example, if the insured gets into an accident and dies after 90 days, most policies with this feature will not pay the double indemnity benefit. This is largely a fear benefit, and not worth the cost.

Is suicide covered in a life insurance contract?

If the policy doesn't specifically exclude it, suicide often becomes a covered life insurance risk two years after you purchase your policy. During the initial two years, if the insured commits suicide, the insurance company normally just returns the premiums but doesn't pay out a death benefit.

My husband of 10 years just died. When I notified his life insurance company, I found out that his first wife is still the beneficiary on his policy! They didn't even speak to one another and I just know he must not have realized that he never made the switch. Is there any way to challenge this?

Unfortunately, this really was your husband's responsibility and it will be difficult and expensive to challenge his mistake. You will have to notify the insurance company of your intent to dispute the beneficiary, and it will be up to a court to decide whether your claim is appropriate, which often requires proving that your spouse was incompetent. This is why it is so crucial that you review your insurance policies periodically and make sure that everything is up to date.

I'm pregnant and my mom is telling me that I need to buy life insurance for my baby. Is this a good idea?

You really don't need to do this. Remember, life insurance is meant to replace income that other people may be dependent on. Your baby has no income and doesn't need her own life insurance. She needs your life insurance, if something should happen to you.

Is it ever a good idea to take out a life insurance policy on another person?

Possibly, if you have a financial interest in that person (usually a spouse or a business partner).

Do you always need to take a medical exam before you can buy life insurance?

Almost always. The major exception is if your employer offers life insurance through a group policy.

If I have a terminal illness, is it too late for me to get life insurance?

In most cases, yes. Major insurers will generally not sell you life insurance under these circumstances, although certain people with HIV may be able to purchase such a policy.

What is a living death benefit?

These riders on life insurance policies, also known as accelerated death benefits, pay your death benefit out while you are still alive, usually if a doctor certifies that you are terminally ill with less than a year to live. The idea is that you can use these funds for your medical care or comfort. This benefit, which may increase the price of your premiums, will also not usually pay you as much in living death benefits as your heirs would have received after your death.

What is a viatical settlement?

This is another expensive option almost exclusively used by people when they are terminally ill. A viatical company will pay you part of the cash value of your whole life insurance policy while you are still alive in exchange for ownership of your policy. They will continue to pay your premiums and they will collect the full benefit after you die. While this is an option if you really need the cash, it really means that you are selling your policy for less than it is worth. Also, it means that you are not leaving your death benefit to the loved ones that you purchased it for in the first place.

My brother and his wife got a second-to-die life insurance policy. What is that?

This type of insurance, which is sometimes called a survivorship life policy, insures two people, usually spouses, and doesn't pay until both insured people have died. This policy is normally worth considering only if you are going to have a very large estate, hence, substantial estate taxes. Of course, this would suggest that you may have enough money so that you wouldn't need life insurance at all, right?

Federal tax law allows you to leave an unlimited amount of money to your spouse when you die without him or her having to pay taxes on it right away. Instead, when your spouse dies, the federal taxes on both your estates come due, and usually must be paid within nine months of the death of the second spouse. A second-to-die life insurance policy could theoretically be used to cover those taxes.

Keep in mind that, as of 1999, federal estate taxes are only due when your estate is worth more than $650,000. Anything over this figure will be taxed at a rate of 55 percent. And this limit will increase annually. By the year 2006, your heirs won't need to start paying estate taxes until the estate is worth more than $1 million. If you don't have this kind of money, don't even think about spending money on this type of policy. Even if you do think that your estate will be large enough to be subject to federal estate taxes, see a good estate-planning lawyer before you make a decision about buying a second-to-die policy. You may be able to avoid estate taxes in ways that make more financial sense for you, such as establishing trusts. (See

Ask Suze . . . About Wills and Trusts for more information about estate planning.)

Is there anything else I need to consider when purchasing second-to-die life insurance?

Ask the agent what would happen in the event that you and your spouse divorced. Is there any provision that allows you to divide or alter the policy? Also, find out what provisions the policy makes, if any, if the estate-tax laws change in a way that would make the insurance unnecessary.

I am 25 years old and single with no dependents. Should I buy life insurance?

You probably don't need life insurance in this situation as much as you need to be saving for your retirement and possibly increasing your disability coverage. On the other hand, the younger you are, the cheaper your life insurance premiums will be, which would be useful if you purchase a 20- or 30-year term policy, if you think it would take you that long to save and invest enough money on your own.

Can I make a trust the beneficiary of my life insurance policy?

Yes. Once your trust is set up, just ask your insurance company what specific language is required when you designate the trust as your beneficiary. (You might, for example, need to designate the name of your trustee, in his or her capacity as trustee.)

Is there any other way to reduce the amount of life insurance I need?

If you are married, you can consider joint and survivor benefits to make sure part of your income will continue to be provided to your spouse. When you retire and are entitled to begin receiving your pension, you will have a series of joint and survivor options, which means that you can choose what percentage of your monthly pension you want your spouse to receive after you die. In exchange, you will have a certain amount of money deducted from your pension checks while you are alive. In other words, if you take a reduced benefit while you are alive, your spouse can continue to receive that payment (or a portion of it) after you die. This can reduce your life insurance needs. (The amount of money deducted from your check will be higher if the percentage of your pension benefit you want your spouse to continue receiving is also higher.)

I'm going to go for the 50-percent joint and survivor benefit for my wife because I figure she'll need about half my income since one can live more cheaply than two. Does that sound right?

That's a very common way of thinking about your joint and survivor benefits but it is actually wrong. Even though your wife will only need to support herself after you die, her cost of living will continue to rise. Also, your death will not automatically cut all her bills in half, right? For example, the taxes on your home, if you own one, will only increase, as will the costs of maintaining the property. Find out how much money would be deducted from your pension check if your joint and survivor benefit was as high as it could be (100 percent) and consider whether you'll really miss the extra money. (Read more about this in *Ask Suze . . . About Planning for Your Future.*)

MISCELLANEOUS

My company has just developed something called a cafeteria plan that gives employees the option to choose our benefits now, including some insurance options. How will this work?

Each plan is different, but generally, these plans offer a "menu" of flexible benefit options for employees. You may be able to choose within a particular type of insurance, such as a standard health insurance plan, an HMO and a PPO, or you may be able to choose among different types of insurance benefits, like life or disability. You generally get a specific number of points or credits that you can use to customize your benefits. You'll need to consider the needs of your family carefully when choosing the form your benefits will take, but you're lucky to have the flexibility. Make the most of it.

My company offers flexible spending accounts, but they seem like a lot of trouble. Are they worth it?

Flexible spending accounts are funds where you can have your employer deduct money from your paycheck on a before-tax basis for you to use to pay for your out-of-pocket medical expenses, like your copayments, and other related health-care expenses, like glasses. This is your money and you can choose how much to have withheld from your paycheck. Periodically, you fill out a claim form with receipts for your covered expenses and reimburse yourself for these expenses. The savings comes because you aren't paying taxes on this money, which can save you hundreds of dollars over the course of the year. The catch is that you do need to submit the paperwork to be reimbursed and you must use all the money you set aside in a given year, otherwise you lose it, so be careful in estimating your medical expenses. If your company offers this benefit, try it out with a relatively small contribution to your fund and see how it feels. You may find that the bit of extra trouble is worth the savings and, as a bonus, it may help you realistically identify how much your medical expenses actually cost you each year, since you're keeping track.

My insurance company is offering to sell me an insurance policy for my mutual funds. How do they work and are they a good idea?
Some companies offer to guarantee that the money you have invested in their mutual funds will be paid back when you die, along with at least a 4- or 5-percent gain for each year that you were invested in the fund, in exchange for either a fee based on a percentage of your investment (usually not more than .5 percent) or on your age. What that means is that when you die, your beneficiaries will get whatever the policy is worth at market rates, and, if it is worth less than the amount guaranteed by the mutual fund insurance, the insurance will make up the difference. This insurance is sort of like a variable annuity, but there are differences, particularly in the way that your gains are taxed. Don't even think about purchasing this type of insurance if you are younger than 55.

When my daughter got engaged, a friend told us about wedding insurance. It sounds silly, but we are spending an awful lot of money on this celebration. Should I investigate further?
Absolutely not. The idea of wedding insurance is primarily that it will protect you if a wedding guest is injured and sues you or will reimburse your unrefundable deposits if you have

to cancel the plans. Your homeowner's insurance and the liability insurance of the reception location should cover any guest injuries. As far as the unrefundable deposits go, wedding insurance doesn't pay out if the wedding is cancelled because your daughter changes her mind. On the other hand, you may find that many of your deposits would be refundable in certain extreme circumstances. You can eliminate the cost of this insurance premium from your wedding budget and not look back.

My daughter is going to be a college freshman in the fall. We got some information in the mail about tuition insurance. What do you think about it?

Tuition insurance would reimburse you for the money you spent on tuition (and, usually, room, board, and fees) if your daughter were to drop out of school before a given semester ends due to illness or injury, in exchange for a premium of about 1 percent of the semester's costs. It's your decision, but I think the insurance is basically unnecessary. Keep in mind that a semester is only three or four months long and that most universities will refund tuition, at least partially, if a student withdraws within the first four to six weeks. Also, if your daughter becomes sick or injured during the last few weeks of a semester, it is often possible to arrange for her to complete her coursework and exams during the following semester at no extra cost (just extra work for her!). If you compare this policy to, say, term life insurance, you'll see that you would be paying a relatively high premium for pretty modest coverage over a short period of time.

You probably think that cancer insurance is a bad investment, too. But there is a history of cancer in my family and I have seen how some of my relatives suf-

fered financially after an illness. This might not be for everyone, but shouldn't I consider this protection?

Of course the last thing you want to worry about when you are really sick is money. But that is why you have comprehensive health coverage! Cancer insurance preys on your fear of cancer, but if you have good general health insurance you should already be protected in case you developed cancer or any other debilitating illness. Why should you pay twice for the same coverage? And if you don't have coverage, why buy narrow protection from only one disease when you could buy expansive protection?

What is a rated policy?

This is a type of policy that may be offered to you if you have some type of unusual risk factor, like a dangerous job, and usually comes with relatively high premiums.

My travel agent always encourages me to buy flight insurance. Do I really need it?

No way. Flight insurance exploits your fear of flying. As you have probably heard before, your chances of dying in a car are much greater than your chances of being in a plane crash. In any case, a good term life insurance policy will cover you in the air and on the ground. Check to see if your life insurance policy has an aviation clause. The credit card you use to pay for your airline ticket may also provide this type of coverage for no fee, so check your membership agreement.

GENERAL INSURANCE CHECKLIST:

- *Compare policies.* Always shop around so that you're sure that you're getting the best policy for your money. Remember that the cheapest policy will not always be the best one for you, because you're not just comparing costs, you are also comparing resources and services.

- *Ask yourself the following questions:*

  Have you read every word of the insurance policy that you are buying?

  Do you understand the definitions the insurance company uses?

  What will your policy cover?

  What will your policy specifically not cover?

  What will it take to qualify for your benefits?

- *Review your policies each year* and make sure that they are still accurately responding to your needs. Did you make major improvements to your house? Did your youngest child finish college? Did your spouse become eligible for Social Security? These types of life changes may mean that your insurance coverage should be changing, too.

ADDITIONAL RESOURCES

National Council on Aging
409 3rd Street, SW
Suite 200
Washington, D.C. 20024
(202) 479-1200

Health Insurance Association
of America
1001 Pennsylvania Ave., NW
Washington, D.C. 20004-2599
Hotline: (800) 942-4242

National Association of
Insurance Commissioners
120 West 12th St.
Kansas City, MO 64105
(816) 842-3600

The State Health Insurance Advisory Program (SHIP)
This is a government program that provides information on Medicare to the elderly and disabled. Each state has its own hotline. You can call (800) 677-1116 to find out which organization you should call in your state for this service.

The National Committee for
Quality Assurance (HMOs
and other MCOs)
2000 L St., NW, Suite 500
Washington, D.C. 20036
(800) 839-6487 or *www.ncqa.org*

The Joint Commission on
Accreditation of Health
Organizations
One Renaissance Blvd.
Oakbrook Terr., IL 60181
(630) 792-5000

Community Health Accreditation
Program (home health care and nursing homes)
350 Hudson St.
New York, NY 10014
(800) 669-1656, extension 242

Finally, primarily for residents of New York, but with some national information, the state's Office of Aging runs something called the HIICA Program (Health Insurance Information Counseling Assistance) which provides New York residents with free confidential unbiased information about insurance. The program has an excellent website with Medigap information at *hiicap.state. ny.us./mgap.*

The hotline number is (800) 333-4114 and is active from 9 A.M. to 2 P.M. Monday through Thursday.

For information on Medicare in English and Spanish from the Health Care Financing Administration: (800) 633-4227. People who require TDD or TTY can call (877) 486-2048.

ASSISTED LIVING

American Assn. of Homes & Services for the Aging
(800) 675-9253, *www.aahsa.org*
Publishes a free pamphlet on senior care options. Also publishes *The Continuing Care Retirement Community: A Guidebook for Consumers* ($10 to $15), available at (800) 508-9442

American Bar Assn. Commission on Legal Problems
    of the Elderly
(202) 662-8690, *www.abanet.org/elderly*
Offers *The ABA Legal Guide for Older Americans* ($13), which includes sections on assisted living.

Assisted Living Federation of America
(703) 691-8100, *www.alfa.org*
Offers a free pamphlet, *Assisted Living Guide & Checklist,* and a listing of member facilities by state; also publishes industry magazine, *Assisted Living Today.*

National Academy of Elder Law Attorneys
(520) 881-4005, *www.naela.org*

A directory ($25) lists attorneys who can review assisted-living contracts. This organization also offers a free brochure: *Questions and Answers When Looking for an Elder Law Attorney.*

WEBSITES

Insurance News Network *www.insure.com*
Independent Insurance Network *www.iiaa.iix.com/default.htm*

INSURANCE RATING SERVICES

A.M. Best (908) 439-2200
Duff & Phelps (312) 263-2610
Moody's (212) 553-0377
Standard & Poor's (212) 208-8000
Weiss (800) 289-8100 *except Florida
     (407) 627-3300 (there are modest fees for quotes with this
     service)

COMPANIES THAT SELL LONG-TERM CARE INSURANCE

CNA (Continental Casualty)	(800) 775-1541
John Hancock	(800) 732-5543
Travelers	(800) 334-4298
G.E. Financial Assurance	(800) 697-1188
Unum	(800) 227-8138
Allstate/LBL	call your local agent

Insurance companies, agents, and policies are primarily regulated by state, not federal, laws. Each state has a department of insurance that is responsible for such regulation. Be sure to consult the department in your state and an expert in the laws of your state when you are making decisions about your own insurance needs.

STATE INSURANCE DEPARTMENTS (800 NUMBERS ARE ONLY VALID IN-STATE)

Alabama	(334) 269-3550	Missouri	(314) 340-6830
Alaska	(907) 465-2515	Montana	(406) 444-2040
Arizona	(602) 912-8444	Nebraska	(402) 471-2201
Arkansas	(501) 686-2945	Nevada	(702) 687-4270
California	(800) 927-4357	New Hampshire	(603) 271-2261
Colorado	(303) 894-7499	New Jersey	(609) 292-5360
Connecticut	(203) 297-3900	New Mexico	(505) 827-4500
Delaware	(302) 739-4251	New York	(212) 602-0429
District of		North Carolina	(919) 733-7343
Columbia	(202) 727-7424	North Dakota	(701) 328-2440
Florida	(800) 342-2762	Ohio	(614) 644-2658
Georgia	(404) 656-2056	Oklahoma	(405) 521-2828
Hawaii	(808) 586-2790	Oregon	(503) 378-4271
Idaho	(208) 334-2250	Pennsylvania	(717) 787-5173
Illinois	(217) 782-4515	Rhode Island	(401) 277-2223
Indiana	(317) 232-2385	South Carolina	(803) 737-6160
Iowa	(515) 281-5705	South Dakota	(605) 773-3563
Kansas	(913) 296-7801	Tennessee	(615) 741-2241
Kentucky	(502) 564-3630	Texas	(512) 463-6464
Louisiana	(504) 342-5900	Utah	(801) 538-3800
Maine	(207) 624-8475	Vermont	(802) 828-3301
Maryland	(410) 333-6300	Virginia	(804) 371-9185
Massachusetts	(617) 521-7794	Washington	(360) 753-7301
Michigan	(517) 373-9273	West Virginia	(304) 558-3386
Minnesota	(612) 296-6848	Wisconsin	(608) 266-0102
Mississippi	(601) 359-3569	Wyoming	(307) 777-7401

INDEX

ABOUT THE AUTHOR

Suze Orman is the author of the #1 *New York Times* bestsellers *The 9 Steps to Financial Freedom* and *The Courage to Be Rich* and the national bestseller *You've Earned It, Don't Lose It.* A Certified Financial Planner® professional, she directed the Suze Orman Financial Group from 1987 to 1997, served as Vice President of Investments for Prudential Bache Securities from 1983 to 1987, and from 1980 to 1983 was an account executive at Merrill Lynch. She has hosted two PBS specials, one based on *The 9 Steps to Financial Freedom* and the other on *The Courage to Be Rich,* and is currently a financial contributor to NBC News' *Today.* She lectures widely throughout the United States and has appeared on *Dateline,* CNN, and CNBC, and has made numerous appearances on *The Oprah Winfrey Show.*

Certified Financial Planner ® is a federally registered mark owned by the Certified Financial Planner Board of Standards, Inc.